A Quilt of

Holidays

Stories, Poetry, Memoir

a Silver Boomer Book

collection compiled by:
Dixon Hearne
Barbara B. Rollins
Becky Haigler
Judy Callarman

www.SilverBoomerBooks.com
~§~
SilverBoomerBooks@gmail.com

Library of Congress Control Number: 2012943619
ISBN: 978-1-937905-19-4

Printed in the United States of America

Table of Contents

"Blessed is the season which engages the whole world in a conspiracy of love." Hamilton Wright Mabie ~§~ "Arbor Day is not like other holidays. Each of those reposes on the past, while Arbor Day pro-

of your Christmas tree. In the eyes of children, they are all thirty feet

Introductory Note

If there is one universal impulse that drives the human spirit, it is celebration. It cuts across all ages, cultures, and nationalities. It reflects in great part who we are. Our calendars are crowded with dates set aside to revel, commemorate – even atone. We yearn to express who we are collectively, to pause from the drone of our daily lives to share special times with friends and loved ones, days we commonly refer to as "holidays."

The word "holiday" derives from holy day, referring to any day set aside for religious observance. Although many holidays have remained linked to world faiths and religion, we have added a number of secular holidays to our calendars over the centuries. Most nations, in fact, pause to pay tribute to traditions and significant events in their history.

The holiday stories, poetry, and memoirs in this book speak to the human heart, make us laugh, and remind us of the importance of fellowship and sharing. From poems of New Year's revelry to tales of Christmas, readers will be treated to a veritable cornucopia of images gathered from the holiday spirits of the writers included in this collection.

We hope you enjoy our "quilt of holidays."

over forty? I live according to twenty-year-old habits." Andre Gide

The Rudolph Sweater

Dixon Hearne

Though the sun ducked behind a bank of gray clouds, where it remained the rest of the week, I didn't complain. The chilly air and cozy comforts brought an early dose of Christmas spirit to our town. Before my very eyes, bedazzled trees sprang up in picture windows, and festive streamers and garlands appeared on busy streets and storefronts. Thanksgiving herbs had not yet faded and dispersed but rather blended into the lively smells of Christmas – cinnamon, clove, peppermint, lemon zest and evergreen resins. It was that wonderful time of year again.

As everyone knew, the annual Christmas Parade ushered in the official start of holiday shopping. We could hardly wait. Right down the center of town came the marching bands and majorettes tossing batons like propellers into the air, interspersed with some thirty colorful floats headed up by the mayor and city council. Old Mr. and Mrs. Stackhouse, always dressed up in western attire, waved "Howdy" from their very own authentic stagecoach festooned with loops of garland tied with silver bows.

Young cowboys in red and green Stetson hats trailed along behind them, twirling their lassos into the hearts and imaginations of onlookers. And the sounds of the season – from Bing Crosby to sing-along carols and kiddy tunes – resonated through the streets. The air was magic with hope and longing. We felt special just to be there, to witness the celebration and to become part of it.

My best friend Scotty and I pushed and tugged and stood our own ground at the front of the crowd for a long while – till a rowdy high school boy decided to shove me headlong into the middle of a marching band. I was petrified!

"Stop still!" a burly band member yelled at me. "Stop and wait till we pass!"

Spectators gawked and pointed, and I froze in place until the drum row finally passed. But quick on their heels was the next float, flanked on both sides by uniformed police cadets, marching lock-step and heavy.

"Up here!" A loud voice called from an enormous float designed like a train engine, with the words *Christmas Special* emblazoned along its sides. "Give me your hand, boy! Jump!"

There was no time to think better of it. I leapt with all my strength and grasped two reaching arms that jerked me onboard as effortlessly as if it had been rehearsed. The crowd began to cheer, flashing smiles in my direction. Even the hateful bully who had shoved me gave me two thumbs up – and instantaneously, I became a sort of parade mascot for the remainder of the long trip down DeSiard Street. Indeed, it would take more than a prank to spoil the parade.

With the passing smiles and hand-waving and voices calling out my name, I felt special for the first time in my life, even famous for a brief moment. I waved back, nervous and awkward, but I knew instinctively it was my moment, a time that would be forever etched in my mind and heart.

As always, the parade would eventually disperse in each direction at Five Points, driven ever forward by the brassy sounds of "Here Comes Santa Claus" from the rear, while Santa and his helpers tossed lollipops to the reaching crowd. Some folks took to the street behind his sleigh and followed to where Santa was quickly spirited away before suspecting children could investigate.

My mother and aunt had waited patiently at Five Points for the parade's end, at which time we were to meet up again. The look of surprise that registered on their faces when they saw me waving from the Rotary float was a bona fide Kodak moment if ever there was one. I got to see the celebration from both sides now – spectator and participant. I would later conclude that I really liked each equally well. It was also the first time I can actually recall being thankful for my mother's insistence on holiday dress. Today, that Rudolph sweater she'd

"Our hearts grow tender with childhood memories and love of kin-

made me wear seemed somehow quite appro-
priate.

No Need for a Card

Sioux Roslawski

a mother never found
and forever lost

a severed DNA strand

empty scrapbooks
pictureless pages
faceless family photos

a canyon
filled with questions
but nothing
ever
comes
echoing
back

arms that can never encircle
or hug or comfort

a wound that will never
ever
totally heal

(oh,
it's scabbed-over now,
but sometimes
it gets picked at
and then it festers)

what is mother's day
like for someone
who's adopted?

are you
sorry
you asked?

Merry Christmas

MaryEllen Letarte

Mandolins play
Exuberant melodies
Resounding adoration in the cold night air
Rejoice! Rejoice!
Yielding to the enchantment of good news

Choirs resonate
Hope
Reminding me that darkness
Is no more
Stars guide my way
Transformation comes through the light of the world —
Magi search the sky and angels sing
Adorned with all that I am I kneel
Seeking sanctuary at the manger

A Most Distinguished Effect

Madonna Dries Christensen

There are as many ways to trim a Christmas tree as there are snowflakes in a blizzard. How you do it probably has something to do with family traditions and rituals from Christmases past.

Some people prefer an eclectic approach, glazing the greenery with colorful ornaments and trinkets collected over a lifetime. Each familiar piece is a stepping stone to an earlier era, evoking a string of memories tied together like the lights on the tree. At the top is often a star or an angel.

Others like a color-coordinated tree, perhaps with only white lights and gold ribbons, or a theme tree laden with Santa Claus figures, snowmen, or miniature toys. One year, in lieu of my traditional eclectic tree, I used an African theme, with carved animals to catch the eye of my granddaughter visiting from South Africa. Breaking with tradition, the tree had no tinsel for the inquisitive toddler to pluck off and possibly eat.

When it comes to tinsel, there are two kinds of people – those who cry, "No, never," and those who claim a tree isn't complete until the silvery threads

Kin Hubbard ~§~ "In the old days, it was not called the Holiday Sea-

are added, "One at a time, please." I'm among the latter; my daughter stands with the former. Still, one year she gave me two unopened envelopes of vintage lead icicles, the kind used when I was a child in the '40s. Dull silver in color, each strand has enough weight so that when hung on the tree, it stays put. Today's flimsy plastic particles create static electricity and float about in the slightest air current.

Humorist Russell Baker shared my appreciation for real icicles. In a column he wrote years ago, he revealed that his wife and children think icicles are vulgar. He explained, "That's the whole point. Of course icicles are vulgar. Christmas trees are vulgar, too, and in bad taste. Putting a chopped pine in the parlor is almost as tasteless as putting a plastic one in the parlor, and the reason we do it is because Christmas is the only holiday we have that author-izes even the fanciest people to revel in vulgarity and bad taste."

Tinsel originated in Germany in about 1620. In the late 1800s, German glassblowers produced crystal ornaments that looked like actual icicles, with a built-in hook for hanging them. In darkened Victorian parlors, trees sparkled with these glass, tin, or sterling silver icicles. Along about 1920, tinsel made from lead was introduced. The product was banned from the market in 1960 to protect children from lead poisoning should they chew on the strands. At that time, Russell Baker bought all the

son; the Christians called it 'Christmas' and went to church; the Jews

lead icicles he could find and hoarded them in his attic.

Alas – I didn't do that, but I have the two packages from my daughter. They originated in Germany, probably in the 1930s. On the brown paper envelope are the words *Brillant Eis-Lametta. Vornehmste a. effectvollste Zierde des Weihnachtsbaumes.* Loosely translated that means "Brilliant ice-tinsel. Most distinguished, fullest effect for your Christmas tree."

Shimmering on my tree, they do indeed create a distinguished effect. Carefully removed and stored each year, they should last another century. And since Christmas is mostly about nostalgia and tradition, perhaps one day my grandchildren will drape my vintage icicles on their trees. They might explain to their children, "We'll do it for Granny. She always put gobs of tinsel on her Christmas tree."

called it 'Hanukkah' and went to synagogue; the atheists went to par–

All Hallow's Eve

Marie Asner

at 5 p.m. my street turns shades of charcoal
spiders start weaving chains of black silk
as the sun fearfully slips away

moon dons red armor
and stands guard by the rock-edged lake

something else is waiting to slowly rise,
slant-eyed along the horizon

dry leaves cover stones by the side of the road
letting the stick man in the fields know
he will be needed soon

lightning trails a whip across the sky
pouting at the slow invitation...

wetlands draw them to the soiree by midnight
those with scales for ears and wings for hands

to go out this night
you need a teacher's pass from beyond

New Year's Eve / Day

New Year celebrations can be traced to the Babylonians around 2,000 B.C. Originally, the new year was celebrated with the coming of spring and the beginning of new life. Developing a calendar to align with the changing seasons and the position of the sun was problematic. Hence, various cultures developed their own calendars. Eventually, the Romans moved the calendar date to the first day of January, a month named for Janus, the god who sees both forward and backward – as symbolized by a two-sided face. It was adopted by many western cultures and remains the most widely accepted calendar today.

Traditions and icons include

- ⏰ depictions of Father Time and newborn babies
- ⏰ fireworks, confetti, noise making, and New Year's kisses

🕛 the Rose Parade and Rose Bowl game on New Year's Day

🕛 gathering in Times Square to watch the ball drop down the pole

🕛 staying awake to welcome in the New Year at midnight

🕛 singing "Auld Lang Syne" on New Year's Eve

🕛 making resolutions, a worldwide practice on New Year's Day

Independence Day In Chicago

Nancy Julien Kopp

Come back with me to the 1940s era in Chicago. During the first few days of July, my younger brothers and I walked to the neighborhood Woolworth's store to buy a very important item for our Fourth of July celebration. We had to make our purchase no later than July 3rd, for all businesses closed on Independence Day.

We walked on the creaky wooden floor, smelling the penny candy lined up in glass cases near the front door. Straight to the back of the long aisle, we found rolls and rolls of colored crepe paper – red, white, and blue, of course. We bought several rolls with money we'd saved. Once home, we stashed our purchase for the next day.

The first thing after breakfast on the Fourth of July, we clambered down the three flights of stairs from our top-floor apartment to the basement where our bikes were kept. Bump, bump, bump – up the steps from basement to courtyard we went with our two-wheeled bikes. Down went the kickstands, and out came the rolls of crepe paper to decorate. We wove the colored streamers in and out of the wheel spokes, and fastened more on the handlebars, then stepped back to see which looked best. Decorating our bikes for America's holiday left an indelible impression of patriotism in us.

Other kids in our building worked on bikes, too. We rode all over the neighborhood, up and down alleys and sidewalks showing off our fancy bikes, not caring how high the temperature might be.

We spent the rest of the day like any other hot, sultry summer day. We ate popsicles to cool off, walked to the park where families sat on the lawn with picnic lunches and waited for the sun to go down. Dad had gone out earlier to one of the only businesses open – the fireworks stand. Money was usually scarce in our family, but Dad always found some extra to buy firecrackers and sparklers for us. No doubt, he enjoyed them as much as we did.

Darkness finally descended over our city, and once again, we hurried down the three flights of stairs – not just kids this time, but our whole family. We gathered in the alley beyond the apartment courtyard along with several other families. Only Dad lit our firecrackers, although I'm sure my brothers wanted to try it. One I loved was a pin-wheel which Dad stuck into a telephone pole. When he lit the fuse, the entire thing whirled round and round, throwing sparks in every direction. Little firecrackers on the ground did nothing but make popping noises, but the Roman candles gave us the real show – big noise and showers of colorful sparks which delighted us. And finally, Dad lit sparklers we held. I loved whirling them round and round, watching the designs the sparks made. All too soon, they burned down to the end and we rushed to get another until the boxes were emptied.

We knew why we decorated our bikes, why people went on picnics and why we had fireworks on the Fourth of July. Our parents talked to us every year about what it meant to have independence and how a war several years before was fought and won to ensure that we lived with freedoms that few other nations had. We grew up knowing there was a serious side to the holiday. Even so, it was a special day we looked forward to every summer.

New Year

Joanne Faries

dismantle Christmas
slam attic door on
Baby Jesus, Santa, and joy

open mailbox to bills.

Fourth of July Fireworks Recipe

Cynthia Gallaher

Spectators on blankets fidget like jumping beans
under the sky's silent blue bowl,
this anxious waiting room awaiting official darkness,
while twilight clings to its last bright hope.

An orange slice in the west dips slowly
beneath a honeyed horizon.
Meanwhile, someone flings a yellow frisbee along
a dusky shore,
or volleys a joke, followed by trails of twilight laughter,

Or throws down one last hand of flashlit hearts,
until something shatters
like a bottle broken
inside a pillowcase.

All suddenly face a new hemisphere,
now glazed in matte pitchness,
where earthbound chefs thickly ladle
spiraling streaks of liquid fire,

Toss multi-colored fistfuls of garden choppings
skyward, and whip gold that cascades like hot butter
between velvety layers, launching ooohs
and aaahs upward from the crowd.

The Redhead and the Tiger Lily

Mary Chandler

Nordic blood coursed through my father's veins 364 days of the year, but not on St. Paddy's Day. That day, he did the Irish proud. Being principal of three elementary schools, he could twist as many arms as necessary in order to gain recruits for the annual St. Patrick's Day program. Kids wearing his favorite color, green, donned costumes and danced or sang their way into his heart.

Not me. I was ten years old, shy, and too embarrassed to perform, even though my long red hair and fair skin made me a natural – not to mention the fact that I probably knew every Irish song ever written. A zillion freckles were the problem. They covered my face like bees on a honeycomb. The slightest kiss from the sun aggravated them. No way was I going to get up on that stage and sing. Not for Dad. Not for anyone.

"Mary," Mama said, her deep brown eyes looking into mine, "Your dad would love to hear you sing."

I shook my head. "Nope."

Never mind St. Patrick. He needed his staff to drive the snakes away. Mama possessed a more

person by the way (s)he handles these three things: a rainy day, lost formidable weapon. Her silvery tongue could have single-handedly charmed those snakes right out of Ireland. Mama wasn't Irish and had never kissed the Blarney stone, but you'd never know it.

"When you sing 'When Irish Eyes Are Smiling,'" she said, "you sound just like John McCormack."

She had my attention. I loved listening to John McCormack.

"I do?"

She nodded. "Each word you sing is full of feeling."

Mama smiled – that kind, warm smile that melted hearts, especially mine. She almost had me, but not quite.

"I'm not wearing a green crepe paper dress," I told her. "Besides," I said, tugging at my pigtails, "I hate this red, red hair!"

Mama's eyes got that faraway, sad look. "Your grandmother had red hair. That's why I named you after her." She brushed her eyes. "She died when you were just a baby, you know. She'd have been so proud to hear you..."

I swallowed hard. "Well, I bet she didn't have a face full of freckles."

"She did, but they faded. Yours will, too."

Not in three days, I thought. I looked away from Mama and stared out the window.

"Will you sing?"

"I'll think about it."

I was practicing the piano after school the next day when I heard a familiar sound. Dad's old Hudson chugged into the driveway. The horn beeped to announce his arrival, and my chubby father bolted out of the car. In his hand he carried a bundle, tied with string. Sprinting across the lawn and whistling "MacNamara's Band," he looked like a leprechaun. Handing me the package, he grinned like one, too.

"What's this?" I asked.

"For your song tomorrow." He thrust his hands into his pockets. "Open it, dear, and try it on for me."

"But I'm not..."

His hazel eyes danced. "It's yours, whether you sing or not."

I tore open the package. Out tumbled a green plaid skirt, a white blouse with green trim around the collar and cuffs, and a kelly-green jacket. I raced upstairs. Putting on that outfit and tying green bows at the ends of my pigtails, I almost forgot about my freckles – until I checked myself out in the mirror. That did it. I definitely wasn't going to sing tomorrow.

Walking down the stairs, I heard humming. Mama and Dad stood by the banister, their voices blending in the old Irish ballad, "The Wearing of the Green." Dad held a beautiful corsage – an orange flower spotted with black.

"What kind of flower is that?" I asked, when the humming ended.

like Christmas on the whole... In its clumsy way, it does approach

"It's a tiger lily and my favorite," Dad said, "because it reminds me of my beautiful freckle-faced, redheaded daughter."

As he pinned the corsage onto my jacket and kissed my cheek, his eyes filled with tears. Mine, too.

On St. Patrick's Day, I danced an Irish jig with my classmates, listened to "Mother Machree," "Peg O' My Heart," "Molly Malone," "Sweet Rosie O'Grady," "Who Threw the Overalls in Mistress Murphy's Chowder?" and "Danny Boy." Then Nedd held my hand and sang "Did Your Mother Come From Ireland?"

I was supposed to look back at Nedd as I sang "When Irish Eyes Are Smiling." I didn't. Instead, I smiled my happiest smile at the dearest "Irishman" in the crowd, my dad, and he smiled back.

Life Was a Cornucopia

Carol Ayer

Our first Thanksgiving together
was a private affair, just us.
We burned the turkey, the potatoes,
and the rolls.
Before we had a chance
to redress the issue,

our elderly neighbor
needed a ride to the hospital.
My new husband,
without missing a beat,
pulled out the car.

My husband engaged the man
in a discussion on the Lakers
as we waited for a doctor.
We gobbled candy bars and potato chips
from the vending machine
until he was pronounced fit
to return home.

Hours later we walked in
our front door;
the clock on the microwave
read 12:03.
Thanksgiving was over,
but I didn't mind.
Life was a cornucopia,
overflowing with possibilities,
abundant with love.

Shepherd in an Old Bathrobe

Elizabeth Howard

I don't want to be
a shepherd in an old bathrobe,
watching the dumb sheep.

I want to be Joseph,
leading a donkey,
talking to the innkeeper,
making Mary a bed in the straw.
Or an angel with wings,
blowing a horn,
making announcements from the sky.
Or a Wise Man in a gold headdress,
riding a camel,
following a star.

But I see a picture of Jesus
in a long robe,
a white lamb in His arms.
"I am the Good Shepherd," He said.

I borrow the woolly lamb
from little sister's bed,
ready to play my part,
shepherd in an old bathrobe.

Valentine's Day

Geoffrey Chaucer is greatly responsible for traditions associated with Valentine's Day. His are the first references to what has become Valentine's Day. He refers to three different Roman tales of romance.

In the first story, Valentine, a Catholic Bishop, helped soldiers marry, in defiance of Roman Emperor Claudius II. For his corruption of the emperor's armies, Valentine was executed on February 14, 270 B.C. The message of sacrifice for love is clearly demonstrated by his actions.

A second story depicts Valentine as a prisoner of Claudius II who fell in love with the blind daughter of his jailer. According to the story, Valentine's own piety and prayer brought sight back to the woman. She was able to read his handwritten note, "From your Valentine." Hence, we have the introduction of love notes and cards to Valentine's Day traditions.

The third story tells how Roman boys and girls were separated until adolescence.

During the festival of Lupercalia, the names of girls were drawn lottery-style by boys, and the couples spent the entire festival together. Many of these pairings resulted in courtship and marriage. This practice also contributed to the present-day tradition of exchanging cards on Valentine's Day.

Traditions and icons include

- ♥ Cupid, the Roman god of love
- ♥ hearts as symbols of Valentine's Day
- ♥ gifts of candy and flowers
- ♥ exchanging Valentine's cards
- ♥ sending poetry and love letters

The Heirloom

Loretta Carter

I reached to the top shelf of my closet to retrieve the large box labeled "Christmas." This was my favorite part of the year, and soon I would have the house decked out with festive decorations, including a six-foot Christmas tree loaded with all kinds of stars, lights and angels.

Christmas was a different story when my sister and I were growing up. The weathered old house we lived in was drafty and damp. The winter snows were chilling and fierce. There was always a roaring fire in the wood heater and a pot of beans boiling on the stove. Plastic covered the windows to keep the cold wind from blowing through the cracks. A worn-out towel or rug was stuffed in the opening under the door.

Mama thought Christmas trees and decorations were a waste of time and money. However, I longed for a tree covered with shiny, blinking lights like some of our relatives had in their homes. The bubbling icicles, silver tinsel, and red Christmas bells fascinated me and kept me longing for things

Dr. Seuss ~§~ "Christmas, children, is not a date. It is a state of mind."

we could never afford. Money was scarce; very little ever came our way.

We always had coconut cake and pumpkin pies baked just in case any of our friends or family came by for a visit. Mama baked from scratch and had a cast iron pan of cornbread in the oven every day at suppertime.

My elderly grandmother, who was half Cherokee Indian, lived in the home with us so my mother could take care of her if she became ill or needed help in other ways. One Christmas when I was around ten years old, I fretted and carried on all week before Christmas, wanting a tree. We knew if there were no tree, there would be no presents, either.

Grandmother comforted me the best she could under the circumstances. She told me the Christmas story about a tiny baby lying in a manger. She talked about the Three Wise Men who followed a star to bring gifts to the baby boy.

As she told the story of long ago, Grandmother threaded her needles with long strings of cotton thread and tied a knot at the end of the string. Her brown fingers, drawn and crooked with arthritis, worked with the skill and ease of an experienced quilter. She was making a string quilt from our old dresses, shirts and any other material she could find.

She cut a square from paper, usually from newspaper or a brown paper bag. This was the pattern she sewed her cloth to, beginning in the center and working outward to the sides. When the square was covered with cloth, she took her scissors and trimmed to the outer edges. Twenty or thirty squares sewn together would complete a quilt top ready for cotton batting and lining to be sandwiched together. Usually these quilts were tacked with yarn instead of quilting.

Slowly, I lifted the box from the shelf, removed the top and opened the wrapping paper. Now I could see the homemade string quilt from years ago. The bright fabric used from childhood clothing brought a flood of memories. It had taken me many years to realize the importance of such a gift. It was more than fabric and string. It was a treasured Christmas heirloom which I enjoyed through the years and displayed only at this special time.

Christmas Cactus

Elizabeth Howard

It used to bloom
on her square table
in the eastern light,
grandmother's white
Christmas cactus.
Now a resurrection
after a long decline,
it is blooming again
on her square table
in my eastern light.

Even They Sing

Jeannette Clift George

The major thing I miss after the Christmas holidays is the Christmas carols. I love them and don't even mind them piped into my grocery store in October. But what I miss is not just hearing them, but singing them. You see, I am not a singer. I am the only person ever turned down for my college glee club! They desperately needed singers for the tour, and I auditioned twice. I was told to join them, but only mouth the words! I am a closet singer, but never warble with the other birds in public.

However, at Christmas everybody sings – singers and non-singers. We all join in! Even my husband, who usually nods to the rhythm of the music, enters full-voiced into "Joy to the World," and together we sing a hearty quartet of "Jingle Bells" (a quartet because I sing in three keys at once). Yes, indeed, in the joy of Christ the King we are all singers!

Maybe that's what God is trying to tell us all year – sing! The prophet Isaiah directs the choir, "Sing to the Lord a new song." I believe each day God gives us a new song with the same music. Sing of Him

"Love came down at Christmas, / Love all lovely, Love Divine; / Love

this day, for you, His precious child, are this very day fully redeemed. I think the saddest grief of the Israelites while being held captive in Babylon was that they could no longer sing the songs of Zion. So sing today and let your freedom ring. The Herald Angels are still singing, so why should the carols stop? Sing the old songs, the time-tested hymns that carry doctrine from generation to generation. And if perchance there are those of you whose singing lacks accuracy of tone and pitch, even if it furrows the brow of those beside you, celebrate with me. Let us shout for joy – in honor of Him for Whom the dawn and the sunset shout for joy – Psalm 65:13. Yes, even they sing!

El Día de los Muertos/All Soul's Day

Cynthia Gallaher

A pot of chocolate melts and
bubbles like mud.
Fresh, sweet corn
releases starch
in a room scrubbed
for *El Día de los Muertos.*
Cooked food
smells wildly of life,

while papier-mâché skulls
look humble, clean,
and angry in their sleep,
shaped for our own
future death.

This afternoon,
a little boy from the Segundo *barrio*
bites into a rock candy skull
bearing his own name.
His soft cheekbones point
at the autumn sun
behind him.
His eyes narrow on his twin sister,
where she stands frozen
to the earth,
dangling a doll.

The night sky is
full of stars,
tips of skeletons' fingers
pressing against dark glass.
All the dead lean toward us,
and trace the outline
of our scissors on folded paper.
Old family stories,
legends how some have died,
make a map on the Mexican heart,
with roads wide and brilliant this night,
by dawn, have zigzagged
in our sight.

The Mistletoe Blues

Sheryl L. Nelms

pictures pop
into my
mind

transport me
back to

high school
years

spent
lusting after

unnoticing
eyes

hung with
green

The Art of Slurping Coffee

Janet Klise

It's not every dad who teaches his daughter the art of slurping coffee.

We were sitting at the chrome and yellow dining room set in the old red house on Backer Street, the weather outside already too hot for a June morning. It was in the mid-1950s, which would have made me about eight years old.

On weekends and school holidays, if I got up early enough, I got to drink coffee with my mom and dad.

Not only was this particular morning Sunday, but it was also Father's Day, and my dad announced that it was time I learned how to slurp coffee. My mother said, "Now, Bill," in what Daddy called "that tone."

It turns out there is indeed an art to slurping coffee. For one thing, the slurping is usually done with vigor and in the privacy of your own kitchen, dad said – where the mixture of air and hot coffee makes it taste all the better.

Then you let it roll slowly toward a swallow, as if flattening a soft piece of chocolate against the roof of your mouth. This way, the coffee reaches every single taste bud.

Daddy insisted that the weakest coffee could be made a little better tasting by a vigorous slurp. But then my dad also said, many times, that there was no such thing as strong coffee, just weak people.

Slurping in a restaurant is much more difficult. It has to be noiseless so as not to attract attention. There were still people in the world who thought slurping coffee was rude, my dad said, but we weren't them. And, of course, the noiselessness made the coffee less improved than a slurp with noise, he pointed out.

You have to hold your mouth "just so," he would say, and the coffee has to be pretty hot. He showed me the "just so" attitude your mouth had to take in order to slurp mightily.

One way you can tell you're ready to slurp coffee with confidence is that you absolutely cannot say the words "just so" with your mouth in the slurping position.

I tried this "just so" position. Then I tested it, posing in front of the bathroom mirror until I thought I was really ready to slurp – without any coaching. That next morning, I waited in the little kitchen of that little house while my mom drank her coffee and tried to wake up and my dad slurped his coffee while reading the morning newspaper.

I took my cup of coffee in my nervous little hands – this was, after all, very important. The coffee was mostly hot milk, but I didn't realize that until a few years later. I slurped. A perfect not-too-loud but effective slurp of coffee.

My dad looked around the newspaper at me. My mom's eyes were suddenly awake. I had passed the test. It was a most marvelous feeling.

To this day, and especially on Father's day, I will stand at my kitchen window and have a few really good slurps of coffee to salute my dad, bless his heart. He gave me the Father's Day gift that year. And I shall always be thankful my dad taught me the fine art of slurping coffee.

New Year's Eve

Kyle McLoflin

With shouts and cheers
and heartfelt hugs,
with roaring laughter
we let go the past —
the good, the bad,
the tears, the smiles —
and grasp at hopes
that lie ahead.

of my favorite times of the year. This is when the whole community and

Kumquats

Sheryl L. Nelms

expensive and
hard to find

in his small
Kansas town

Gramps had
them every
year

for Christmas

bought them
as a treat

said they
reminded him

of the 1920s when
he lived
in

Miami

St. Patrick's Day

St. Patrick's Day is a special day set aside to honor a man who chose to forgive the people of Ireland who persecuted him and deprived him of his freedom. According to known records, St. Patrick was born Maewyn Succat in Great Britain. He was abducted by Irish bandits at age sixteen and taken to Ireland, where he was forced to work as a herdsman. After six years of slavery, he escaped to France where he spent several years preparing to become a Roman Catholic priest. During this time, he had a dream in which the people of Ireland were reaching out, grasping for his helping hand. This, he thought, was a divine sign and a special calling to return to Ireland to convert its people from pagan practices to Christianity. Patrick's efforts were rewarded and his influence spread across the land. Legend has it that St. Patrick used the power of God, rather like Moses, and drove all the snakes out of Ireland. Another legend holds that he used three-leaf shamrocks in his teaching to symbolize the holy trinity.

The association of leprechauns with St. Patrick's Day has nothing to do with St. Patrick or his teachings, nor does the wearing of green.

Traditions and Icons

 St. Patrick's Day parades

 leprechauns

 wearing something green

 displaying and wearing shamrocks

 searching for four-leaf clovers, symbols of good luck

 drinking green beverages (natural or dyed)

 singing Irish songs, such as "Danny Boy" and "My Wild Irish Rose"

Konawa in Time for Christmas 1928

Judy Callarman

Every Christmas season during all my growing-up years, my parents and my brother Jim and I got around to talking about Christmas miracles. Jim and I always urged our mother, Mary Dorcas Green Sitton, to tell us again the story of how she learned the real meaning of Christmas when she was twelve, her family living through some hard times in Konawa, Oklahoma. She could fascinate us with the tale, waving her hands about, her large brown eyes shining. This is her Christmas story in her voice, the way she told it to us every year.

I heard my mother talking as I got close to the barn. Her voice sounded urgent and disturbed, different from her usual happy talking and singing. Alarmed, I peeked through a crack in the wall.

I saw her kneeling beside a bale of hay. Little specks of hay and dust floated in a sunbeam shining through one of the cracks. Mom's dark homespun skirt was wrinkled in a heap as if she knelt down in a hurry and didn't care about it. Her hands were clutched together on the hay bale; her eyes were closed, and her upturned face was covered with tears. I stayed quiet. I knew Mom was talking to God.

"Oh, God, how will I take care of all these children? Please help me."

My heart felt stabbed. I didn't want her to know I had intruded on her private moment with God, so I hurried away. I knew how hard it was to feed all of us, especially since my father's death two years before, when I was ten. We often went hungry.

But I knew, too, that she loved all eight of us and intended to keep us all, even though my aunt and uncle pestered her to give them my sister Maggie. Aunt Bertha would say to Mom, "Eula, you have eight big, strapping kids, and we don't have any. Your life would be easier if you'd just give us Maggie. We'd give her a good home and you'd have one less mouth to feed."

"I may have a hard time," Mom would say, "but I'd never give away one of my kids. I don't have any kids to spare."

We all worked hard on our farm near Temple, in southern Oklahoma. We grew all our own vegetables and had a few apple and peach trees. When we needed meat, we butchered a hog or a calf and cured it in the smokehouse. We made our money growing cotton. Even the youngest, John and I, had cotton sacks we were expected to fill. Some years my brothers Cotton and Duck had jobs on oil rigs, and my sisters Lois and Elsie could work at the B&O Cash Store in Temple. But when the Depression loomed, none of us had jobs. Everybody around Temple was hungry, like us.

Mom decided the best thing to do was move to Konawa. I thought about her prayer in the barn when we heard about some jobs there. She said she wasn't worried; God would provide for us. "We'll be settled in Konawa in time for Christmas," she said.

In Konawa we were able to rent a pretty white house, small but clean, within walking distance of town, a church, and our school. Hope lifted our spirits, especially because Christmas was coming, even though we were still hungry most of the time. Even if no money could be spared for gifts, it was a time of love and joy. Mom made sure we understood that we celebrated the gift of our Savior's birth at Christmas, and that was much more important than any other Christmas present could ever be.

A few days before Christmas, the children of Konawa were invited to a Christmas party at the nearby stone church with stained glass windows. I was the only one of my family who wanted to go, so I walked to the church by myself that afternoon. The air was cold but still, and through the trees I could see the church steeple. The scent of wood burning in fireplaces gave me a cozy feeling as I skipped along. I told myself, I belong in Konawa already – things will be better here.

The big fellowship hall was crowded with children. Some of them talked and laughed in small groups; I thought maybe their families belonged to the church. I stayed back near the wall with some girls I had met at school. Many of us, I noticed, were quiet and big-eyed, amazed by the beautiful Christmas tree decorated with red and green paper chains and stars. Next to the tree, a large table was piled high with net Christmas stockings, each filled with apples, oranges, nuts, and bright red and green ribbon candy. My underfed stomach growled.

A pretty lady dressed in Sunday clothes came out from somewhere and read us the Christmas story from the Bible as we sat cross-legged on the floor. Then she led us in singing some Christmas carols. I was eager for one of those stockings – I could almost taste the crisp apple and the juicy orange.

A smiling man with red cheeks and gray hair joined the lady, and together they handed out the stockings to us children. But a terrible thing happened; they ran out of stockings before they came to me. I wanted to cry and beg for one – but I didn't say anything. I just left the church and walked home as fast as I could. I didn't tell Mom or my brothers and sisters because I didn't want Mom to feel bad. I kept thinking about her prayer in the barn, asking God how she would take care of all of us. I could tell Christmas that year was going to be a big failed expectation. The season of joy and giving had just turned dark and dingy and hungrier than ever.

Two days later, Mom, Elsie, Maggie and I walked home from a window-shopping trip to Boone & Styron's Department Store. Seeing all the holiday finery downtown made me feel bitter and even more deprived.

As we came up the sidewalk, we saw a big box sitting on the porch next to our front door. Mystified, we opened it, and we could hardly believe what we saw. The box was packed full of food – a huge turkey, sacks of flour, sugar, and cornmeal, eggs, beans, onions, potatoes, jars of canned fruit and vegetables, and even a big chocolate cake. My sisters and I gasped with surprise and delight, and Mom's eyes filled with tears.

"Lord have mercy," she whispered, wiping her eyes. "Help me carry this inside."

We unpacked the box, piling up all the food on our dining table. Our spirits soared. It was a miracle. Christmas came in spite of my disappointment at the church party, in spite of poverty and hunger. We had a wonderful Christmas dinner and plenty of food to last at least a week.

We never found out who left the box of food, but we were deeply grateful to them and to our God for such thoughtful people. I have not forgotten how awful I felt, being left out when other children received gifts of food and I was hungry. But neither will I ever forget how I learned that God's loving spirit lives in the hearts of people, the real spirit of Christmas giving.

"I told you God would provide for us," Mom said. "He always does."

Moving In – Memorial Day, 1955

Janet Klise

On this day of hurried walking, bending, stacking,
    pushing, shelving,
dusting and cleaning, the flag goes up first.

We're put outside under the elm and out of the way.
Judy falls asleep, but I'm seven and older and too
    fidgety.

The back yard is not familiar; it's not comfortable.
I see too many trees – what kind are they, anyway?

There are too many rose bushes – why aren't
    they blooming?
And too much dirt; it's all dry sand.

There is too much sky, wide and a hazy blue.
Too much to get used to.

I turn an ordinary-size brown bug into a two-toned
  greasy spot.
It takes less than three seconds.

I frantically rub, slap and slash, cleansing the
  guilty index finger
of the sticky remnants of death, leaving the
  remains on the old yellow blanket.

Now I think about the poor bug's family.
Surely bugs have families, just as I do.

I see amber-colored scenes of the bug's small
  lean-to house,
propped up against a tree root, with a pair of
  boots on the porch.

Mother bug is cooking dinner and wonders why
  her husband is so late.
How much did he gather today?

Junior and Sister bug are playing on the flaxen
  rug in front of the fire place,
waiting for the sound of their father's six feet on
  the front stoop.

Was he a soldier in his little world like my dad was
  in mine?
Did he march behind his flag with dignity and pride?

I cry for his family, for the Mother and Junior and
  Sister bugs,
and I fall asleep on the soft, warm blanket under
  the sharp valley sun.

Annual Tangerine

Wilda Morris

The tangerine—
as round in my hand
as balls hung on the tree,
its skin like the family
which held me together,
its golden pulp a memory
of love and candles.

Each Christmas
bells rang and carols
filled the church.
I strode to wooden manger,
a shepherd or angel
in bathrobe or belted gown.
I laughed aloud, clapped
joyful hands to greet
the ho ho ho,
bright red suit.

Santa planted
in my hand
a bag of candy and nuts
and one juicy tangerine.

Passover

One of the most widely-observed Jewish holidays, Passover is a festival commemorating the Exodus of Israelites from slavery in Egypt. It begins the 15th day of Nisan in the Jewish calendar, preceding Easter in the Christian religion in the Northern Hemisphere. According to history, the Israelites were instructed by God to mark the doorposts of their homes with the blood of a spring lamb and, upon seeing this, the spirit of the Lord knew to pass over the first-borns in these homes. The Christian observance, Maundy Thursday is rooted in the Jewish feast of Passover.

References to the original Passover feast provide instructions as to how the meal is to be eaten: "with your loins girded, your shoes on your feet, and your staff in your hand; and ye shall eat it in haste: it is the Lord's Passover" (Exodus 12:11). The Seder meal is performed in much the same way by Jews all over the world.

Traditions and icons include

- ψ celebrating for seven or eight days, depending upon whether a sect is Orthodox or Reformed
- ψ ritual Seder meals, consisting of roasted lamb shank bone, roasted egg
- ψ *maror* (bitter herbs, often horseradish, *charoset* (sweet salad), *karpas* (parsley or dill)
- ψ *chazeret* (bitter herb, often romaine lettuce), salt water, *matzah* (unleavened bread), and wine (or grape juice)

Easter Bloomers

Terri Elders

On my sixth birthday, in the summer of 1943, Mama confided to my older sister Patti and me that there was a baby on the way – I knew it would be a boy. Despite Grandpa's teasing that I'd soon have a baby sister, I had faith. I fully intended to remain the official "youngest daughter" for life, though I was perfectly willing to play the dual role of "big sister."

So when Joel was born on September 30, I was not surprised. But when he arrived home from the hospital, I was somewhat disappointed. A new first-grader, my favorite activity was playing school. I had been counting on this new family addition to join me and my dolls in my makeshift schoolroom. Baby Joel couldn't even sit up, let alone hold a pencil in his tiny fist. Mama comforted me, though, by painting a rosy picture of the future when Joel indeed would become my attentive pupil.

So I bided my time, helping bathe and diaper him, joining Mama in singing "Tura-Lura-Lural" to him at bedtime, admiring him when he finally could eat a peanut butter sandwich by himself. I waited for him to walk. I waited for him to talk. And finally at the age of three, he began to join in playschool sessions.

But sometimes Joel didn't seem to take his lessons seriously, so as his teacher I would inform him sternly that while the dolls were earning A's, he'd be lucky to get a C. "It's C, A, T," I would pronounce, pushing back my bangs in exasperation.

"T, A, C," Joel would spell back, and then giggle and clap his hands. "Better than the dolls, huh?" I would throw up my hands in disgust.

Joel was equally cheerful in his Sunday school class, and talented, as well, particularly excelling at coloring Bible story pictures. Then one Sunday as Easter neared, I overheard his teacher telling Mama that Joel would have the first line to recite in the group's recitation of a holiday poem. His opening line would be "Easter lilies blooming remind us of the day." The other preschoolers would in turn complete the additional three lines of the quatrain.

At dinner that night, I confided my fear that Joel wouldn't get the line straight. That's when Grandpa promised to help coach, an idea which immediately alarmed me. A perennial tease, Grandpa recently had turned his attentions to my innocent brother. Spaghetti, Grandpa claimed, was made from the worms that inhabited the garden. Joel no longer ate pasta. Grizzly bears roamed the hills above our home and feasted on wild blackberries. Joel no longer helped pick berries.

And the first line of the Easter poem, I heard him assure Joel, really was "Easter bloomers waving."

Determined that Joel would not disgrace the family by garbling his line, I set up a counterattack. As soon as I memorized my own Easter poem for the service, I began drilling Joel. "It's 'Easter lilies blooming,'" I would insist. Sometimes he would get it straight and sometimes he would give me Grandpa's version. I decided to call upon divine reinforcement. "Remember," I would threaten, "If you don't get this right, Jesus will be disappointed."

When we awoke that Easter morning our baskets were already at the foot of the bed. I remember savoring first the sweet, chewy yellow marshmallow Peeps chicks. As I got dressed, I downed a rainbow-hued hard-boiled egg, chewed a stick or two of Wrigley's Juicy Fruit, and gazed several times into the innards of my chocolate diorama egg. I counted my jelly beans and offered to trade Patti for the black ones, my favorite. From time to time, I would glance nervously at Joel while Mama adjusted the collar of his sailor suit.

Then we went to church. Patti was the first of our family to perform, her alto soaring on a solo interval during the choir's rendition of "The Old Rugged Cross." I was next, reciting my poem, and then taking a seat in the front row to watch as Joel's preschool class marched on stage. The congregation chuckled as the toddlers jostled one another to get into line.

Finally, Joel stepped forward confidently. "Easter," he announced, and then paused. His eyes caught mine, and then flickered left towards Grandpa near the end of the pew. "Easter," he began again. I held my breath. "Lilies," he enunciated clearly. "Blooming," he continued. "Remind us of the day." He grinned his jack-o-lantern grin. I beamed back. The next child stepped forward.

Grandpa grumbled a bit on the way home, but I held Joel's hand and told him he would be getting an A on his next report card – and a gold star, too. Then I leaned over and whispered that I knew that Jesus was pleased.

"Did I do better than the dolls?" he asked.

"Oh, yes," I said. "That's better than anybody in my class."

Even now Joel still chides me that I'm the over-achiever, the "doer," the academic one in the family, always busy trying to teach, to mentor, to influence. That's certainly true. But what he overlooks is that as my first pupil, he indeed proved to be my teacher, teaching me the delights of watching somebody learn and succeed. He also taught me to persist and persevere – and to appreciate the efficacy of the subtle threat.

Artichokes

Carole Ann Moleti

I make a confident turn left onto Westchester Avenue and negotiate between the stanchions under the elevated subway tracks of the Number 6 line. After about three blocks, I realize the grocery store is in the other direction and smile. Grandma Clo wants me to take a spin past her apartment, just to be sure I don't forget anything.

Twinkling holiday streetlights do nothing to brighten the drab, windswept cityscape – or my Christmas spirit. No snow is in the forecast to mask the reminder that, almost ten years ago to the day, her coffin was lowered into the ground a few miles from here.

I idle in front of what used to be Grandma's kitchen window, brightened by sunny yellow curtains. Now there are bland, off-white blinds, closed tightly against my intruding eyes...eyes desperate for one last glimpse of garish sunflower wallpaper, and of the gray-haired lady in a housedress, curls dampened by fragrant steam rising from pots on the stove, standing at the kitchen table rolling dough, making meatballs, or stuffing artichokes.

Longfellow ~§~ "As we express our gratitude, we must never forget

I come back to my old Bronx neighborhood to shop, to recapture the special moments. And besides, it's the only place I can get the queer, spiny vegetables in enough quantity for an intimate Christmas dinner for the twenty-four of us left.

It used to be forty: a marathon of cooking and baking, three generations making a glorious mess in the kitchen, and a lot of happy noise before setting a feast on the dining room table. Divorces, including my own, fractured the togetherness. Distance and feuds separated cousins. Illness and death intruded, picking off grandparents, aunts, uncles, and parents one by one.

That can't be undone by lingering here. I make the right turn and am lucky enough to snag the last spot in the teeming parking lot of *Bonavita* – Italian for "the good life." An octagonal cardboard pit is surrounded by elderly Italian women eager to share secrets like why female artichokes are better than males and how to tell the difference. I get a glimpse of life long ago, as the women picked them right off the plants in hillside gardens around Grandma's ancestral coastal village, Trebisacce.

I listen politely, always happy to learn something new. But I follow Grandma's sage advice – they should be small or the hearts will be too tough. My own heart aches, missing her as she must have pined for the family and friends she left behind.

"They're so dear," one woman murmurs as she loads about a dozen artichokes into her cart.

that the highest appreciation is not to utter words, but to live by

I look toward her, expecting, hoping to see Grandma again. She used the same expression to complain about the cost – a sacrifice for her family while living on Social Security and a widow's pension.

"Yes, they're very expensive this year." I feel a connection with this woman, a cosmic bond, but she's not Grandma Clo.

I fill my cart with an equal number of females and males, before trundling down the aisle to pick up other ingredients for the antipasti. While in the check-out queue, I swim in memories of chicken soup loaded with orzo and tiny meatballs, savor the flavor of a stuffed pepper, munch a salad minced into tiny pieces, hand tossed and perfectly coated with oil and vinegar.

In Grandma's later years, when pushing the shopping cart full of flour and sugar and gallon tins of olive oil was too much, I'd bring them to her. She'd make me lunch, and then we'd go buy a wreath at the stand near the cemetery.

Grandma knew exactly where Grandpa Frank's grave was, even though there were no landmarks to help it stand out amongst the rows of other headstones. She'd cry and say her prayers while I tied the wreath on the black granite monument. Then we'd go back to her house, have coffee and dessert, and get busy.

She complained about how tired the cooking and baking made her, but didn't want my help – just company. I watched, trying to master the techniques while her reddened hands with cracked nails, fingers knobby with arthritis, stubbornly kneaded bread dough.

On the last Christmas she was well, I found a moldy container of her signature breadcrumb mixture in the refrigerator. I dumped it into the garbage, but she didn't notice.

Grandma, confused and distracted, struggled to remember the recipes. I tried to reconstruct them by reading her notes, but nothing tasted right. Artichokes are the one thing I've been able to perfect by experimenting with her scribbles on grease-stained paper.

The sharp leaves pierce my skin and shred my cuticles as I trim the stem and hard tips. I spread the leaves apart before immersing them, upside down, into the breadcrumb mixture. They have to be packed tightly into a pot for hours of steaming.

Grandma insists they must sit, at least overnight, for the flavors to meld. I re-heat them, counting on the fragments of her magic trapped in the encrusted blue-black enamel pan for the finishing touch.

When I peel off the leaves one by one, scraping the soft central portion loaded with pungent, flavorful stuffing against my teeth, I savor every happy memory of my childhood. When I finally dig deep down to the tender heart, which melts like butter in your mouth if they've been carefully prepared, my heart melts, too. The aroma of olive oil, the bite of imported cheese, the tang of garlic, the whole experience brings me back to when life was simple and family was the most important thing in my world.

The heap of discarded leaves, like a collection of treasures ravaged by time, reminds me to savor special moments while they're tasty and alive, not tattered remains.

At the dinner table I ask, as Grandma Clo always did, "How are the artichokes? Enough garlic?"

Could it be Grandma, speaking through me, exhorting me to do my best to hold the family together and pass the traditions down to my children? She's buried deep within the earth, but is with us at those moments.

Every Italian in the neighborhood is in the store tonight, it seems. I revel in the familiar slurred Neapolitan dialect. The manager surveys the bustling scene.

A satisfied grin spreads over his face. "*Buon Natale a tutti.*"

Was he the same man she used to barter with, in the old village tradition, to get a better price? Or is that man, from a time long ago when things were different, gone too? The cashier finishes bagging. I swipe my credit card.

There is still one item on my to-do list. I drive to the cemetery, buy a wreath, and lay it on the moss-covered headstone that now bears the names of both my grandparents. Grandma Clo's smile pokes like a ray of sunshine through the clouds as I say a little prayer and assure her I'm keeping up with things the best I can. Life is no longer simple, and family is not the only demand on my time. She understands.

I leave, in a hurry to get busy cooking, and won't make a wrong turn on the way home.

April Fools Day

Joan Peronto

After three days of summer
two months early,
the guest that lingered near the door
has stepped back in, snow in his hair.

My daffodils bend earthward
to listen to the grass Indian style.

Easter

Easter is the day when Christians cele-
brate the resurrection of Jesus Christ, as
recorded in the Bible. It is also celebrated by
some cultures as a non-religious holiday that
derives from pagan customs related to spring.
Some traditions that spring from these cus-
toms include Easter bunnies and egg hunts.
In short, Easter is a combination of pagan
traditions, the Jewish celebration of Pass-
over, and Christian beliefs. It may surprise
some Christians to find that some of our
Easter traditions existed before Christ was
born.

It is commonly accepted that the origin of
the name "Easter" came from the records of
St. Bede in the 8th century. He proposed that
the name Easter came from "Eastre," the
goddess of spring and fertility. According to
pagan myths, Eastre was appeased by
symbols of new life. Hence, eggs and rabbits
both became symbols of fertility and renewal.
Similarly, the Greeks believed that Perseph-
one, goddess of spring, returned to earth

once a year to replenish the land. Over time – and with the conversion of Romans to Christianity – spring festivals became meshed with religious observances, resulting in present-day practices and traditions.

Religious traditions / icons include

- ✝ Stations of the Cross, a Roman Catholic tradition retracing Christ's last day
- ✝ Maundy Thursday (Last Supper celebration)
- ✝ Good Friday observance, the day of Christ's crucifixion
- ✝ Easter Sunday celebration, the day of Christ's resurrection from death

Secular traditions / icons include

- ✝ Easter egg hunts, Easter bunnies, and baskets of candy and treats
- ✝ Easter cards and gifts

The Christmas Puzzle

Susan Sundwall

No single day of the year takes so long to pass as Christmas Eve – especially for small children. This thought came back to me recently as I re-stacked some old puzzles in their tattered boxes while cleaning the small attic room in our very old house. I had to smile because the puzzles repre-sented a tradition in our family – one that came about without deliberation or precedent.

We'd been in our new home for less than a year when Christmas rolled around back in 1978. Our three boys were young, in a new school environ-ment, and we were all making our way as best we could in the community. We'd made some friends through school and church, and my husband and I were delighted to be asked to a small gift exchange at one family's home. A few weeks before the party, we'd drawn names, and it was exciting to be a part of it all. I don't remember what gift we gave, but I vividly remember the gift we got – a puzzle.

This was no ordinary puzzle; it was comprised of two characters, Adam and Eve, drawn as small cartoon characters over and over on the face of the puzzle. It was all in black and white. The attraction of it was the cute sayings, such as Adam quoting to Eve the command to go forth and multiply. This he did while winking, and, as the puzzle got passed around the room, a lot of the men winked, too! I didn't think we'd ever put it together, but I thanked the giver and we partied on.

What I didn't figure on was the love of puzzles residing deep within my husband. A few days before Christmas, he set Adam and Eve on the kitchen table. Soon the two older boys were helping, and I think the slightly risqué sayings were part of the allure. But I didn't fuss too much because, lo and behold, peace had descended! Now I could get on with my wrapping and baking and all the crazy last-minute things that the holiday requires.

The following year, another friend from the group gave us a different puzzle. "You seemed to enjoy the one last year so much," she said. This one had packages of Lifesavers as the theme and the kids loved it. They eagerly tried to piece together the cherry and butter rum sections, as they jostled for the best vantage point around the table. It wasn't long before we all took up the challenge and had the candy puzzle done by the end of Christmas Eve.

That puzzle was followed by others I bought myself, because I'm no dummy. I liked the distraction it offered, and the kids were beginning to think of it as our own family tradition. After several years,

all the flaws in our human relationships: it is the feast of failure, sad

we began to get fussy. No puzzles with solid-colored big-sky borders – too hard. No puzzles under 500 pieces – too easy. The puzzles that were just right were the ones that had well-defined sections like the one I found with a dog bakery. That was a hoot. The doggy treats, the doggy baker and the bakery itself were just about perfect. In each subsequent year, I had to search diligently for puzzles that met our high standards. It was one holiday chore I didn't mind.

We've been in the same community for many years now, and our Christmas Eve puzzle is legendary among friends and family. Some of them will join us for an eggnog and try for the best seat at the table where the puzzle waits. One or two have pocketed the last piece to be whipped out later for that "aha" moment of triumph that finishes the picture. Soon we began getting the puzzle out a few days early when there was too much snow or stress to deal with. A troubled mind often finds solace in turning a bright piece this way and that – the motion of hands indicative of working out a deeper, more personal problem. And a bit of competition among brothers to find every piece that finished the bakery dog's face made their mother smile, too.

Once, when our boys were teens, we set up the puzzle a whole week ahead of schedule. This one was just the right size for the coffee table, and, if I remember correctly, was all about colored eggs.

One evening my husband and I were off to an office party and permitted a few friends of the boys to come over. Guess what they did? They finished that puzzle. It would have been okay, except that the look on my husband's face when he saw the completed masterpiece told a different story.

"They finished the puzzle," he said sadly. "I was kinda hoping to work on it some more."

If that doesn't testify to the success of one of our favorite family traditions, I don't know what does.

But now, these many years later, looking at the old puzzle boxes, I have to acknowledge that sometimes traditions die. Children grow up, head to college, marry. The important thing is that there was a tradition, and keeping that tradition – for however long – fosters good memories and outweighs whatever material treasures we could give. A case in point was the year our eldest son married. I'd been bustling around making special snacks and treats, wearing myself out, as usual. Barely had I finished my preparations and gotten myself cleaned up when he and his wife walked through the door. In my daughter-in-law's hand was a box which she handed to me, smiling. Pictured on the cover of the puzzle box was the fattest, reddest, jolly old Santa Claus I'd ever seen.

"It's a puzzle!" I said, hugging her.

"Of course," she said, "after all, it's the family tradition."

It just doesn't get any better than that, does it? Maybe in the years to come, we'll revive the tradition. After all, we now have grandchildren to think of.

Flag Day Thoughts

Nancy Julien Kopp

A hard-won American flag
waves in blustery Kansas skies,
untouched by evil enemy hands.
No foreign silver saber rips into its
splendid stars and stripes, no gun tears
gaping holes in the red, white, and blue.

Hold dear the freedom won with flag held high.
Wave the unfurled banner from coast to coast.
Sing the songs, beat the drums, blow the bugles,
whate'er it takes to spread the patriot's creed.
Then carry freedom's flag deep within your heart.

Thanksgiving is:

Sheryl L. Nelms

the fat pop of
boiling cranberries

cornbread dressing and turkey gravy
pumpkin pie piled with whipped cream

frost on the windshield

pheasant hunting
deer tracks in green wheat
flocks of migrating geese honking overhead

the scent of a mesquite
wood fire in the Franklin stove

our nondenominational
interracial

diversity day of appreciation
for another
chance

In Search of Excellence

Diane Tarantini

I stood and faced the ten people gathered around our dining room table and held up my pointer finger.

"Will you excuse me a minute, please?"

I bolted upstairs, buried my head in a laundry basket, and screamed. When I lifted my head, there was my husband's pant leg.

"Something wrong?"

I glanced up from my crumple.

"It's not perfect."

He shrugged. "It doesn't have to be. It's excellent. That's enough."

Last year my Thanksgiving hoohah was a bit of a fiasco. I decided to be cool and brine my bird. Nowhere in the directions did Martha Stewart say it would take the turkey three times longer to roast due to its forty-eight-hour soak in salt water.

Thankfully, all the guests were polite about the extremely delayed entrance of the main course. We actually started out fine. The wassail was perfect, all simmery and cinnamony in the Crockpot I'd embellished with fall foliage paper. It made the house smell as if it had one foot in November, the other in December.

The appetizer buffet was stunning. I had to smack the kids' hands with a wooden spoon to keep them from spoiling their appetite with shrimp butter on toasted baguette slices. My ma-in-law and I vied for the biggest glutton title with the *Bon Appetit* spiced pecans. And thanks to dear husband, the roasted bell pepper and havarti slices on fancy crackers disappeared in five minutes flat.

When the oven timer buzzed, I clapped to get everyone's attention.

"And now for the main event," I said. "Give me a few minutes to get the turkey out of the oven, and we'll get this feast started for real."

My husband hoisted the steaming Tom Turkey out of the oven and onto my Granny's cream ironstone platter while I got the side dishes squared away. Nutty green beans go in this bowl. Garlic mashed potatoes will live in there. These two trivets will hold my sister-in-law's best-ever-she-won't-give-me-the-dang-recipe sweet potato casserole. And I'll fill our wedding anniversary bowl with my modified *Gourmet* magazine stuffing recipe.

I balanced on tiptoe to peek over my husband's shoulder as he sliced into the bird's breast. I squealed. He jumped. The carving knife clattered on the stove top.

~§~ "Most Texans think Hanukkah is some sort of duck call." Richard

I waved my arms frantically. "Stop!" I said. "The juices aren't running clear! The Butterball package said the fluids can't be pink or cloudy."

My husband glanced from me to the bird. I pressed potholders into his hands.

"Quick! Put him back in the oven."

I increased the heat twenty-five degrees and used my Nan's giant wooden spoon to shove the roasting pan all the way back and left it there. I crammed the side dishes onto the racks, hoping to keep them warm, too. I stood, smoothed the front of my cute aqua and lime Anthropologie apron, and headed into the dining room with a basket of cheddar pecan biscuits in one hand and a crystal bowl of salted Amish butter in the other.

"Everyone get a biscuit and butter. It'll tide you over 'til turkey time."

My husband checked the bird thirty minutes later. He leaned against the dining room doorway and shook his head ever so slightly. I choked on my biscuit bite, wadded my pilgrim-and-Indian print napkin, then threw it at my empty plate.

"Here. Let me take a look."

My mother-in-law followed me into the kitchen. She touched me lightly on my shoulder.

"Why don't we start with the side dishes?" she said. "While the turkey finishes up. It'll be fine."

I sighed. And sniffed. "Okay."

Lewis ~§~ "Now the feast of unleavened bread drew nigh, which is

She removed everything from the oven but the turkey, then arranged the serving dishes on the kitchen table. I placed a little calligraphied placard in front of each side item. The guests filed in, heaped their plates, and returned to the dining room.

Before we dug in, my oldest brother prayed. "Lord, we thank you for this bountiful array of food. Bless it to our bodies, and please, comfort my sister in her time of distress."

A half hour later my husband inspected the turkey, then once more after twenty minutes.

"Think I'll wait an hour before I look again," he whispered to me before he sat.

I took a swig of white wine. "You know what? Just leave it in there 'til it's black for all I care."

My mother pointed her fork at me. "Actually, this is good for my hiatal hernia," she said. "Small amounts of food throughout the day are much easier to digest than large meals."

I tried to smile. "Thanks, Mom. That makes me feel so much better."

When we were done with our stuffing and veggies, I stacked my plate on my husband's and stood.

"Forget about the turkey," I said. "I'll give everybody some to take home. Who's ready for dessert? There's praline pumpkin pie or frozen caramel pumpkin torte – both with homemade hazelnut whipped cream."

In the kitchen I flipped the toggle on the coffee maker and sliced five pieces of each dessert and dolloped them with whipped cream.

My husband placed a cup of coffee on the kitchen table in front of me. I started to take a drink, but stopped. I inhaled, then wrinkled my nose.

"What's in it? It smells different."

He grinned. "A shot of Bailey's," he said. "I thought you might need it."

I felt my nostrils flare and my eyes start to burn. He patted my back.

"There, there. Think excellence, not perfection."

I turned to face him, my hands on my hips. "This won't happen next year."

He cringed. "We eating out?"

I snorted. "Heck, no," I said. "I'm gonna cook the dang turkey the day before."

Dinner Theater

Carl Palmer

into the menu smiling
cheeks reflect candlelit
white tablecloth islands
amid the carpeted scurry
of busboys and waiters
in the backdrop of our night

tinkling laughter and ice cubes
accompany depths of conversation
overheard yet unheard
from couples in quorum
around the raised platform
at the center of the room

noises diminish with
dimming lights as
all eyes are drawn
to the spot center-stage
except mine
which remain upon you

Happy Valentine's Day, my Dear

Mother's Day

According to ancient Roman tradition, the annual festival "Matronalia" was held to celebrate Juno – goddess of childbirth. Husbands presented their wives with gifts and offered prayers. Another Roman tradition that has found its way into modern culture involved ceremonies for Cybele ("Mother of the Gods"). With the advent of Christianity, the rituals were altered to include the Virgin Mary. This was the beginning of what came to be known as "Mothering Sunday" in England.

By the 17th century, Mothering Sunday in England had become an annual day for workers to break from their labor to return to the "Mother Church" in the town that they called home. This event took place on the 4th Sunday of the Catholic observance of Lent. This religious respite from work also provided a time to visit family (in particular, mothers). Among the customs that quickly took root were the giving of gifts and flowers and pampering mothers on their special day.

The first reference to Mother's Day in the United States appears on a historical placard in Albion, Michigan. According to the back story, on the second Sunday of May, 1887, a Mrs. Juliet Calhoun Blakely took the pulpit to replace her church's reverend, who was unexpectedly called away. According to the story, her sons were so inspired by her courage and delivery that they vigorously urged others to honor their mothers on that day each year.

Anna Jarvis is credited with the formal establishment of Mother's Day in the United States. She petitioned the governor of West Virginia, and on April 10, 1910, he proclaimed the second Sunday of May as Mother's Day. From this grassroots effort, the celebration became a national matter when President Woodrow Wilson signed a bill that officially added Mother's Day as a national holiday.

Traditions and icons include

- family gatherings and celebration
- Mother's Day cards, gifts, and flowers
- treating mothers to nice restaurants
- performing special favors for mothers

Dad's Last Thanksgiving

B.J. Yudelson

"Thank you for Mommy and Daddy and teddy bear."

"I'm thankful for my Legos."

"I'm thankful that my teachers are nice this year."

"I'm grateful to be here with my aunt and uncle and cousins."

"I'm thankful for my good health and family."

And so it went, Thanksgiving after Thanksgiving. Before we dug into the turkey and trimmings, each person at our table expressed gratitude for whatever seemed most precious. For decades, my sister and I alternated years between her New Jersey home and mine in Rochester, New York. Wherever we were, we could measure our children's growing maturity by what they found most important.

Once our children were grown, and we were spread out from Boston to Los Angeles, it was harder to bring the families together for the holiday weekend. "Let's do Thanksgiving in Rochester this

or modern, is very simple: loving others. Come to think of it, why do we

year," I suggested to my sister the year that our father turned 92.

"Do you think your older boys would come?"

"You can count on George and me, and Aaron. I hope Dan and Jon will, but I don't know."

After convincing Dad that he and Martha, his bride of six months, should fly to Rochester, I sent out an email to all his descendants. When they heard that Granddad would be there, they all accepted. As the days grew shorter and colder, Dad wasn't sure he was well enough to travel. I called my sister again. "What if he dies in Rochester?" we asked each other. "Then he'd go with his boots on," we agreed. "He'd be surrounded by all his family. What could be better?" At the last minute, Dad almost didn't come.

"But you have to," I persuaded. "You're the reason that everyone else is making the trip." Later he told me that he finally decided that if he were to live even a few more weeks or months, he'd kick himself for having missed this chance to be with his children, grandchildren, and great-grandchildren.

I saw how our dad, Joe, beamed when he held his namesake, Joey, born six weeks previously to my son and his wife, and I knew I had been right to insist. All told, twenty-seven of us, including infants, a fiancé and a girlfriend, paid homage to Dad's greatest treasure: family love. I was delighted with how well we respected each other's differences in eating preferences (kosher, vegetarian, and no restrictions) and lifestyles.

At Thanksgiving dinner, the youngest generation – at least those old enough to talk – gave thanks for best friends and toys. The grandchildren, however, were acutely aware that they might never see their grandfather again. Each one in turn offered special thanks:

"I'm thankful to be here with all my family and especially with Granddad."

"I'm happy that I've had Granddad in my life for so long."

"I'm thankful that Martha has brought so much happiness into Granddad's life."

"I'm grateful for Granddad's love and generosity."

Dad wiped his eyes, tried to speak, and gave an embarrassed grin instead. We didn't need words to appreciate his loving gratitude.

He died four months later, Martha and his daughters at his side. I'm thankful that he made the effort to join us for his final Thanksgiving. Dad gave each of us one more memory, one more blessing, one more reason for gratitude.

be celebrated in the school room with pine trees, tinsel and reindeer,

Shepherd

Wilda Morris

One small shepherd
escapes, sneaks through
the side door
to the sanctuary

gazes with worried eyes
at the filled pews
till he finds
his father's face.

He waves and returns
to the pageant cast
with courage to go on
when it's his turn.

First Footing

Cathy Bryant

For those with Scots blood, New Year's Eve (or *Hogmanay*) is a very important holiday, more so than Christmas in many ways. Of course, everyone goes out and drinks a dram or two of good whisky, but there's also another custom, which my family observed every year. It's called the "First Footing," and we all had to be home for midnight so that we didn't miss it. One year it all went very differently, and I'll tell you about that in a moment, but this is what happened most years.

When midnight struck, we all called out, "Happy New Year!" and drank a toast, and then linked arms and sang "Auld Lang Syne" like anyone else. But then we all sat down and waited in front of our Yule fire.

Soon there'd be a loud knock on the door.

"Shall I answer that, maybe?" my mother would say casually, and my father would answer, just as casually, "Aye, ye might as well, then."

"But who is it?" my little brother Alistair would ask, as he was very young, and had either been asleep or failed to remember on previous years.

"You'll see!" I whispered.

So my mother would go and call out, "Happy New Year to ye, whoever ye be, and come in and welcome!" and fling open the door.

And in would come Uncle Jim. The tradition stated that it had to be a dark-haired person, and there were very few in our red-headed family, so it was always Uncle Jim. He'd be holding a sack, and he'd bring it into the lounge; then he'd pull things out of the sack, one by one, with a theatrical flourish.

"I bring you bread, that this year will never find you hungry!" Then he'd bring out some hot rolls or bannock cakes, fresh and still warm from the oven.

"I bring you money, that this year will never find you poor!" Then out would come strange and lovely coins for the children to touch and gaze upon wonderingly: ancient silver sixpences, tiny old farthings with robins on them, or strange foreign coins in square or triangular shapes, or with holes in the centre.

"I bring you coal, that this year will always find you warm!" he cried, and would bring out a lump of black coal. But being my Uncle Jim, he always had to do something a bit more exciting than that. He'd fling the coal into the fire – together with a sneaky handful of flash or flare powder, so that there'd be a great WHOOSH! and a silver flash, and everyone would *Ooh!* and *Aah!*

And finally Uncle Jim would say, "I bring you greenery, so that this year will bring you all long life and good health," and he would bring out a plant. Sometimes he managed to find the most amazing blooms out of season. One Hogmanay, he brought night-scented stocks, which filled the room with a heavenly smell. They are in the back garden still.

A number of years ago – quite a large number, so I won't say the exact amount – we had one of "those Decembers." You know the kind: Everyone is ill, or feuding, or absent, or in love and therefore zombified. And there's a power cut or a leaking roof, or some other disaster every time you think it's all okay and you'll finally be able to sit down and relax with a cup of tea.

We got through Christmas somehow, and we were looking forward to Hogmanay when the latest blow fell. It was December 30th (or as Alistair called it, "New Year's Eve Eve"), and we were baking in the kitchen when the phone rang. Uncle Jim was in hospital – he'd been adjusting some Christmas decorations and fallen off the stepladder, and his leg was broken in three places.

Well, we dashed to the hospital and made a great fuss of him and did as much celebrating and commiserating with him as we could. But he was going to have to stay in hospital, as his fracture was complicated. It didn't occur to us until we got home that of course he wouldn't be able to do the First Footing.

"Who's going to do it then?" asked Alistair. "It has to be a dark-haired person."

"Never mind this year's," said mother wearily. "It's just one of those times. We'll enjoy it all the more next year," and she began to rescue things from the oven.

"You're dark-haired, Catherine," Alistair whispered to me, his eyes wide and hopeful.

"But I'm only thirteen!" I hissed back.

"That's awfu' old," retorted Alistair, which I expect it is, when you're seven.

Despite my protest, I was desperate to do something to cheer everyone up, so I made a plan.

Just before midnight on Hogmanay, I excused myself and very quietly slipped out of the house. Looking back, this was emphatically not a wise or sensible or safe thing to do, and I was very lucky not to come to harm. I managed to carry out my plans, and found myself back on my own doorstep just as midnight struck.

I heard all the choruses of *Happy New Year!* and the clink of glasses and the singing of "Auld Lang Syne" – I could hardly bear to wait. But then I heard my mother say worriedly, "Where's our Catherine?" and I knew that my moment had come.

I knocked heavily on the door.

My mother didn't say anything, but opened the door anxiously. When she saw me, her face changed rapidly from worry to relief and then anger. But when I said, "Don't I get a fine First Footing welcome, then?" she stepped back and smiled ruefully at me.

I didn't have a sack, but rather a large carrier bag. Still, I did my best to be as theatrical as Uncle Jim. I walked into the lounge with my head held high, and called for silence. The room went quiet and everyone stood still, eyebrows raised.

Dinner had been a bit rushed and stressful, so I thought my first gift would go down well.

"I bring you bread, that this year will never find you hungry!" I said, and brought out hamburgers in buns, with fries for everyone.

Well, they all laughed, but also thanked me and ate, and the air was warm with the smell of food.

"I bring you money, that this year may never find you poor," I said. "Well – sort of." And I brought out a piece of paper. "Mum, this is a copy of the IOU I gave to Mr. Harris at the burger bar. Credit is a form of money, isn't it? And he says could you pay him as soon as possible, please?"

Everyone fell over laughing again, and I got a round of applause. At that point, all the lights went out.

"Oh, not another power cut," sighed my father.

The only light now was the great fire. But there hadn't really been a power cut – I'd whispered to Alistair to turn off the lights for the next part.

"I bring you not coal, but fire itself, so that this year will find you warm and bright!" I declared, lighting a sparkler and waving it about. I handed them 'round, and everyone obligingly drew pictures and names in the air, and smiled in the glittery light.

Then I realised that I'd made a mistake.

"Oh, I also brought you greenery, so that the year will keep us healthy and long-lived. But it was supposed to go with the burgers," I explained, crestfallen, and held out the packets of salad.

Well, everyone declared that a refreshing salad was exactly what they felt like most, and munched away stoutly, which was very kind of them.

Then Mother explained that we hadn't planned a First Footing at all this year, what with Jim being ill, and my father said how proud they were of me. I was given a further round of applause and some good highland whoops and some claps on the back.

When we next went to visit Uncle Jim, he was much tickled by the tale of my first go at the First Footing. He said we should do it together, or take turns in the future. So now we've had many happy years of planning the First Footing together, with all sorts of peculiar gifts and other mischief.

Uncle Jim was in his fifties then and is in his eighties now, which gives you an idea of how old I must be. Over the years it's been a little frustrating just how stubbornly red-headed the rest of our clan has been. But last year I got my dearest wish – Alistair's lovely wife Kirsty gave birth to twin boys, both with shining dark hair like myself and Jim. I shall have some training to do!

Punxsutawney Phil

Barbara B. Rollins

You never bother to come down south
yet at least your handlers claim your gift
to guess the weather way down here.
It seems a crapshoot, right some wrong some,
but some years right as rain. Annals reflect
a shadow-sighting the thirty-third day, 1910.
Chillicothe, Texas, fourteen hundred miles away,
huddled bundled against blizzard winds,
keeping small-town folk from getting there
the day my grandparents said their vows.

Crewel Knots at Christmas

Remembering M.H.

MaryEllen Letarte

Each year you return
in the ornament you stitched.

We see the wounds
that crisscrossed us all.

We see your lustrous hair,
your unlined eyes.

We could not hold you here,
your babies nor your friends.

Your last knot tied us to your youth,
left tears that will not mend.

We see your hand-stitched knots
secure on this ornament – unlike you –

You swung free.

Memorial Day

Memorial Day, also known as "Decoration Day," is celebrated annually on the last Monday of May in the United States. It is a federal holiday set aside to honor those who died to defend their country against its enemies. The observance originated at the time of the Civil War, as a way of paying tribute to so many fallen soldiers.

Decoration Day was originally observed only by northern states. In 1873, it was formally accepted as a legal holiday in New York. In the coming years, an alternative name, "Memorial Day," was floated and eventually took hold. Animosities lingered in the air long after the Civil War, and southern states honored their dead on different dates.

The name "Memorial Day" was given greater attention on June 19, 1926, when the United States Congress declared "Memorial Day" as a federal holiday. It expanded the purpose to include the honoring of fallen soldiers from all wars. Since that time, it has become a symbol of unity among all Americans. While the practice of placing flowers on graves is historically common practice, President Lyndon Johnson officially declared Waterloo, New York, as the birthplace of Memorial Day in 1966 – the 100th anniversary of the first recorded memorial observance.

Traditions and icons

- observing the National Moment of Remembrance (3:00 P.M. local time) Arlington National Cemetery
- family gatherings and picnics
- prominent displays of American flags at half-mast
- parades and ceremonies
- decorating gravesites of fallen soldiers

A Clatter of Hooves

Kerry Alan Denney

She heard the clatter coming from outside. Although he tried to rein them back and quiet the warning bells, in the silence of the packed drifts of snow glistening in the twinkling starlight even the softest nicker or neigh carried – especially so late.

He was coming back later every year. She didn't mind. She loved him so much. No one else could ever give so much of himself and expect and receive so little in return. His rich rewards were the insatiable love for fantasy he inspired and the knowledge that there was always great need for his services.

Every year there were more hopeful little dreamers needing him to help make those dreams come true. It was the same every year; it had been that way for as long as she could remember. And though some who came before her may have found the monotony maddening, she drew great comfort from it. His job was exhausting and dangerous, but she loved him more with every year that flew by for his steadfast dedication to it – and to her.

maybe his father was right, he usually has a son who thinks he's

She sighed, threw the afghan off her legs and stood, her knees popping. She hated to abandon the toasty fire, but this was important. If nothing could stop him from completing his rounds, then by God and all that reigned over creation, nothing was going to stop her from greeting him after his arduous journey – and making him comfortable again at home.

She shuffled toward the front door, her legs and feet protesting the cold. It didn't matter that he would be weary. He would still greet her with his rumbling chuckle, still win her heart with his rosy cheeks when he smiled. She lived for it.

It didn't matter if the curse lasted for a thousand years; she would remain by his side, because love withstood time. And she knew he loved her as much as he loved every one of his little charges, as much as they all loved him, too. She loved him more than that, because he had made the ultimate sacrifice with his pledge to her, and to this arduous duty.

She smiled as she approached the door, knowing the crew was already taking care of the animals and guiding him home through the blankets of sleet and snow, home to her. She heard the soft crunch of hard frost as she touched the doorknob, and her heart fluttered again, just as it always did when he finally returned. Though they were both old and gray, their love kept them youthful and occasionally spry enough to keep the bedroom as warm as their kitchen and their hearts.

wrong." Charles Wadsworth ~§~ "I stopped believing in Santa Claus

She opened the door, and her breath caught in her throat. He staggered toward her and fell into her arms, and she barely kept her footing as she dragged him inside. She leaned him against the door frame and gazed into his twinkling eyes.

He gave her the smile, and though it was weak, it held the promise he'd always kept.

She closed the door, shivering from the frosty breeze that kept worming its way into their bones with the determination of the alpha-omega lifecycle that ruled the mortals. Soon it would be time to brave the challenge and get back to work, but for now, it was time for comfort, and a reminder of their inseparable bond.

She took a deep breath, wrapped his arm over her shoulder, and practically carried him over to the chair in which she'd just been sitting – hoping it still bore some of her body heat. It was getting harder each year to warm him up after his trip.

He chuckled as she helped him settle into the chair, and he kissed her on the cheek before she rose.

"Long night, sweetie?" she asked, knowing the night had lasted nearly forever. She turned to the fire, added some hickory logs, and stoked it. The crisp wood caught almost instantly, sending a fragrant blaze of warmth into hearth and home.

"Nothing I can't handle, my love," he said, and stretched his snow-crusted boots out on the ottoman.

when I was six. Mother took me to see him in a department store and

When she got the fire roaring again, she smiled and turned to him and lovingly removed his boots. She set them beside the fire, and when he smiled at her again and held his hands out to her – those rosy damn cheeks just glowing – she fell into his merry eyes all over again, and drifted back into his loving arms.

They cuddled, and she rubbed her cheek against his, feeling the softness of his snow-white beard and moustache tickle her and send tingles up and down her spine. It was still just like the first time she sat in his lap.

"I think, my dear," he whispered in her ear, making her tired old immortal heart flutter yet again, "that it's time to settle in for a long winter's nap."

"Yes," she mumbled. Finally, it was. There would be time enough again, and it would come far too soon, to prepare for next year's trip. For now, it was their time.

"Would you care to join me, my love?" he asked, and she trembled, remembering every Christmas that came before, and the love that came with it. Nobody else quite knew how to share love like her jolly husband.

"Yes," she whispered, and kissed him.

She rose and smiled at him, wriggled her fingers, and he took them and stood beside her. They hugged, and it melted the remaining icicles that worry and fear had frozen in her heart.

Apparently it had been another successful trip, because she felt his strong heart beat against hers.

She squeezed him, cherishing the feel of his arms around her. He kissed her again, and finally belted out his hearty trademark laugh. She giggled, loving the way his ample belly jiggled just like a bowl full of jelly.

In only another three-hundred-sixty-four-point-two-five days, it would be time to load up the sleigh again. Everything would be chaos again, frantic elves scrambling everywhere, trying to meet the deadline.

But for now, the night and the long winter were theirs to share.

Easter

Kyle McLoflin

A holy day —
the world alive
in shades of yellow-green and
the yawning buds of Easter time,
a restless world floating
on the strength of promise
and a covenant of renewal.

Christmas Pageant

for Florrie

Wilda Morris

Joseph sat in silence by the manger
where baby Jesus lay
wrapped in white bands.
Mary showed all the excitement
of young motherhood,
kicked her fragile, palsied legs,
waved stiff arms.
Joy rose from deep within her —
eyes sparkling, smile broadening,
she giggled,
waved and kicked strongly,
then laughed aloud
and in that family called church,
joy spread. It was said,
never has there been a happier Mary.

Plain and Simple Hearts

Madonna Dries Christensen

From my childhood in 1940s Iowa, I recall grueling winters that seemed endless. Valentine's Day broke the monotony of waiting for spring. As soon as Valentine cards appeared in the window of the Ben Franklin Five-and-Dime, my younger sister Shirley and I hurried in to make our selections.

Back home, we sorted our cards, choosing the appropriate verse for the teacher and for each classmate. We were careful about the messages on the cards for boys. "Valentine Greetings" was safe, but "Please Be Mine" would give a boy the impression we *liked* him.

When I was in fifth grade, I came home from school one day and Ma greeted me with this announcement, "I got a bargain on Valentines. This big package for only a dollar."

That she had chosen our cards was bad enough, but when I saw them, I knew Valentine's Day was ruined. The cards had no lacy frills, no lollipops stuck in slots, no crinkly hearts that unfolded when you opened the card, no Cupids aiming arrows. There were no messages such as

"My love is great, my heart is true, and both I offer now to you." The bargain package held plain construction paper hearts, perhaps a hundred of them, each about three inches in diameter.

"They're simple, but pretty," Ma offered.

I knew enough not to voice my thought: *Yeah, simply awful and pretty dreadful.* In a household with a passel of kids, economy came first.

I pouted as Valentine's Day drew closer. Ma suggested pasting the red hearts onto lacy white paper doilies, or adding pictures of flowers or birds cut from magazines. I wrinkled my nose. That would make them look even more homemade. Reluctantly, I addressed the hearts and laid them aside. The next morning I sulked off to school and deposited my pitiful offerings in the decorated box by the window.

For the holiday party, Miss Klein brought heart-shaped cookies and we had chocolate milk instead of white. When Miss Klein asked who would like to be postmen (one girl and one boy), I didn't raise my hand. I didn't want to deliver my lowly declarations of friendship. Then, because the hearts were small and had no envelopes, I worried that they might have fallen to the bottom of the box and would go unnoticed by the postmen. It would be awful if that happened and the kids thought I hadn't brought any Valentines at all.

Not to worry, the plain red hearts began showing up among the fancy cards accumulating on desks.

Chatter and laughter filled the room as children read verses aloud and teased one another about secret pals and boyfriends and girlfriends. I glanced at my cards, but I would wait until I got home to read the verses. Shirley and I always played Valentine store; we gathered the cards from all us kids, spread them out on the table and pretended to purchase them.

When the dismissal bell rang, and I headed for the cloak room to get my coat, a red-haired, freckled-faced boy stopped me and said, "Your Valentine was the best one I got."

Taken by surprise, I wondered if he had sensed my feelings about the plain red hearts and was only being polite. Or, did he *like* me?

I hurried home, eager to read my cards and see what the message on my Valentine from Fred would reveal.

Halloween Fear

Pat St. Pierre

In the middle of the night
Scratch, scratch, scratch.
Attic boards squeak
Sounds get louder.
Ghosts aren't real;
My heart is thumping.
A squirrel in the rafters?
Too loud – maybe a mouse.
The noise gets louder,
Downstairs a scraping sound.
Afraid to move, but must get up.
Tiptoeing around the room
To switch on the light.
Down to the kitchen
To look around.
The "hanging" kitchen witch
Put there for Halloween
Moves in the breeze.
Her broom scratching on
The side of the window.

Flag Day

Flag Day was adopted to commemorate the acceptance of the new American flag by the second Continental Congress on June 14, 1777. It is also a day to acknowledge and reflect upon the challenges faced by America's forebears in their struggle to become a united country. Prior to the Revolutionary War, most colonists flew flags of their motherland, particularly Great Britain. In its quest to become a separate sovereign nation, colonial leaders recognized the need for purely American artifacts and symbols. Legend holds that Betsy Griscom Ross was asked by the Continental Congress to stitch together a flag it had designed. She did so, and it met with resounding approval. In colors of red, white, and blue, the flag featured stars and stripes. Each of the thirteen horizontal stripes represents one of the original colonies; white stars on a blue background represent the states of the union. In 1949, President Harry S. Truman signed into law a Congressional act that officially added Flag Day as a national holiday.

Traditions and icons

- prominently displaying the American flag
- local and national parades
- singing of patriotic songs, such as "America the Beautiful" and "The Star-Spangled Banner"
- reflecting upon the American flag and its importance

Sunrise Service

Janelle Burch

Sunrise Service was a unique annual event that bonded our small community together. The banks of the Mississippi River provided the backdrop for the scenes that unfolded on Easter morning. As the rising sun reflected off the slow-moving waters, a mist rose behind the props set up for the performance.

My eyes were heavy as we arrived at the levee where people from surrounding communities gathered to witness and become a part of this event. I could feel the cold early-morning breeze through the warm coat and blanket wrapped around me.

The familiar sound of the wavy record on the turntable signaled the beginning of the service, and the static reassured me that this was the same soundtrack from years past. The levee looked different on Easter Sunday. Makeshift bleachers were set up along the slope. The structure built for "The Last Supper" stood empty all year, waiting for this day when it would be equipped with table and chairs to accommodate Jesus and the twelve disciples. The players passed around bread and wine as Jesus looked at each of them and gestured, while the voices on the phonograph articulated the dialogue of this reenactment.

The grassy area beside the tomb became the Garden of Gethsemane, where the disciples lay sleeping while Jesus prayed. And this scene quickly broke up when Judas arrived with the Roman soldiers; he silently pointed and watched while they took Jesus away. I knew that three large wooden crosses lay hidden behind the concrete ledge at center stage, even though they were not visible until the crucifixion scene. Soon we would see Jesus and two thieves raised into position against the backdrop of the river. Jesus would be taken to the stone tomb, where the door would be closed. We learned to hold our ears as a firecracker would explode the moment the door burst open and Jesus left the tomb to appear to Mary and the disciples. And that was the end.

The sun was higher in the sky, the grass was slightly wet from the dew, and the crowd was amazingly quiet as we walked down the levee road to return home. Many years later, I heard people reminiscing about that wonderful pageant. I remember my reluctance to wake up so early and go out in the cold. When I realized this pageant had become a thing of the past and would never be a part of the Easter celebration again, I missed it.

My sisters and I fondly reminisced about the crackly-sounding record, the predictability of the

local citizens in their acting roles – and our antici-
pation of each scene, each action and verbal
exchange. Though lacking the professionalism of
local theatre productions, the Easter Sunrise Ser-
vice served a great purpose on its own merits. It
brought the Easter story to life, touched many lives
and provided a memory which many have not had
the chance to experience. Those who may not
have found their way to church on Easter morning
had the opportunity to celebrate and to take with
them the gift of the Easter season.

The stone structure with an open doorway that
served as the tomb is the only prop that remains,
most likely a mystery to those who knew nothing of
the annual service. This is an appropriate reminder
of the risen Christ and a tribute to the group of
people from different churches in the community
who gave their time and effort to create a meaning-
ful, memorable experience for at least two genera-
tions. How fortunate are those who hold memories
of celebrations such as these. They renew and
refresh us as we continue on our journey.

Texas Turkey Tango

Barbara B. Rollins

A multicultural family
on both lines of the blood,
with maternal or paternal parentals,
Aggies denigrated tea-sippers
while Longhorn loyals spewed Aggie jokes.
Mounds of potatoes, "egg gravy" —
with and without the eggs —
pink salad, cornmeal dressing,
pound cake and pecan pies —
with and without pecans —
piled on china plates replenished often
served to tranquilize the masses
and hold the hostilities to verbal jabs
come kickoff.

The Secret Ingredient

Debra Ayers Brown

"Santa's coming tonight!" Daddy rushed inside from the cold North Georgia night, closed the door with his shoulder and dropped a bag of navel oranges, nuts and stick candy beside me on the floor. A box of Moon Pies, my favorite treat, rested on top.

I sat cross-legged in front of the crackling fire and stared up at the tall, broad-shouldered man with thinning hair and engaging smile. Even at eight years old, I realized that Daddy, a hard-working man of few words, was an unlikely Santa. I also knew from past Christmas Eves that we'd deliver toys, clothes and candy to a neighbor who Daddy said needed our help.

"It's almost nine o'clock," he said as I grabbed the Moon Pies, anticipating the joy of biting into the chocolate-covered cookie sandwich with the marshmallow filling. "The presents for the Reynoldses are bundled up in the back of the truck."

I followed him to the kitchen to find Mom.

"Just in time to add the secret ingredient," she said to me and slid the first of four cake layers onto a plate, then stuck holes in the layer with a pointed knife.

As I had done for the previous two years, I spooned on a bit of juice from two oranges and watched it seep down into the cake. "There's no cake as good as Sara's," I repeated, just like everyone at her office said about her baking. Mom smiled, and I ran my finger over the mixer beaters, scooping the sugary icing into my mouth. "Yum," I murmured.

Mom iced the cake, and I retrieved the bowl of freshly grated coconut.

"Okay, it's ready to go," Mom said after sprinkling on the last of the coconut.

"What?" My mouth flew open.

"We're giving it to the Reynolds family."

"Not our cake?"

"Giving to others is what Christmas is all about," Dad said.

"But Mom can't make another one before Christmas," I said. "Can't we slice it and save some for us?"

"No." Mom placed cellophane lightly over the cake.

"Let's go," Daddy said, buttoning his jacket. He pulled my new wool coat from the peg by the back door and handed it to me. Mom carried the cake. I grabbed my box of Moon Pies and stepped outside.

The winter wind stung my face. I tucked the box under my arm, buried my hands in my pockets, and dashed to Dad's old, battered '56 Ford pickup that in no way resembled Santa's sleigh.

I slid across the cold vinyl seat. Mom settled beside me.

"Why doesn't Santa deliver their gifts?" I asked. Mom glanced at Daddy.

"The Reynolds' children don't believe anymore," she said.

The old truck bounced over the bumpy roads. I stared at the cake jostling on Mom's lap and hugged the Moon Pies to my chest. Maybe if they believed, we'd be able to keep our cake. I fumed as we stopped in front of the small wooden house. A single bulb burned on the porch, leaving the rest of the house dark and remote. A dog barked in the distance. I shivered and hoped they weren't home.

Daddy hopped out, eased the door shut, and left us in the truck. His work boots crunched across the frozen ground to the porch. The truck's heater whirred, but my breath still froze in the night air like smoke from a cigarette.

Within seconds Daddy returned with Mr. and Mrs. Reynolds.

Mr. Reynolds, the tallest and skinniest man I had ever seen, opened the door and leaned inside the truck. "Hello, ma'am," he said to Mom.

The dim light threw shadows across his thin, drawn face. He pushed back a lock of black hair from his wrinkled forehead. Dark, bushy brows framed eyes sunken into his head like a skeleton's.

"How are you, little one?" He extended a hand across Mom to me.

"Fine," I said and shook his bony, calloused hand. I remembered Daddy saying that he was an excellent carpenter when he was able to work. Even in the shadows, I could tell he was sick. One night I'd heard Daddy telling Mama, "He's a proud man. He refuses to go to the hospital because he doesn't have the money to pay for it."

Mr. Reynolds backed up two feet and stood by his wife, a woman half his height dressed in a flowered cotton housecoat and a pink, threadbare sweater.

Mom stepped out of the truck and handed the cake to Mrs. Reynolds. They huddled together talking.

I clutched my box of Moon Pies and peered out the window.

Mr. Reynolds met Daddy at the back of the truck, accepted the bags of gifts from him, and started toward the house. After a few steps, he stopped and let the bags fall to the ground. He turned around and walked back to face my dad.

I watched, spellbound.

After a few moments of silence, he said, "These toys and that beautiful cake –" He choked back tears. "Now we won't have to disappoint the children. We'll have a special Christmas celebration like we used to have." He wiped at his eyes with both hands. "I don't know how to thank you." He threw his arms around my dad and hugged him.

Daddy patted his back. "It's what Christmas is all about," he said, clearing his throat.

Mr. Reynolds nodded and picked up the gifts. A tear rolled down Mrs. Reynolds' cheek as she joined him.

"Wait!" I jumped out of the truck. "Take these," I said. "Everyone loves Moon Pies." I handed the box of my favorite treat to Mrs. Reynolds.

Daddy put his hand on my shoulder and squeezed. I climbed into the truck. Mom slid in beside me and cupped my hands in hers. My heart pounded against my chest. But now I understood why Daddy wanted to help Santa even if no one knew but us.

Daddy's giving heart showed me that God would provide all we need so that we would be able to share with others. From that moment, I believed in using the power of love and concern to give hope to others. Like Daddy said, "It's what Christmas is all about."

Advent

Judy Callarman

O come, O come Emmanuel
Voices echo rich tones,
hushed ancient words,
children red-cheeked.

Candlelight in windows —
warm quickened breath,
frosty in cold darkness,
catches in anticipation.

Incarnation of Spirit
shall come to thee
Spirit of love
Rejoice rejoice

Father's Day

Father's Day is celebrated on the third Sunday of June in the United States. It is a day set aside to honor and to show respect for dads. The first recorded story advocating the creation of a special day for fathers comes from Grace Golden Clayton of West Virginia. In 1896, her father, along with 359 other men, was lost to a mine explosion near her home. A special service for fathers was held at the Methodist Episcopal Church on July 5, 1908. Inspired by the story of Anna Jarvis and her campaign to establish Mother's Day, Sonora Dodd of Spokane, Washington, sought and obtained official sanctions for local celebration of fathers.

In 1924, President Calvin Coolidge publicly supported a Father's Day holiday, leaving it to the discretion of each state. It wasn't until 1956 that Congress passed a resolution to officially recognize Father's Day. In 1972, President Richard Nixon signed into law the permanent annual obser-

ing out of the self to one's fellow man that makes giving worthy of the

vance of Father's Day to be celebrated on the third Sunday of June.

Traditions and icons

- family gatherings and celebration

- lavishing fathers with gifts, cards and attention

- treating fathers to nice restaurants

- picnics, barbecues, and cookouts

In Keeping with Christmas Past

Madonna Dries Christensen

The Salvation Army's holiday donation drive is a long-standing tradition. The unobtrusive manner of the workers and the merry tinkle of their handbells are all it takes to make me reach into my pocket. In addition to the familiar red kettles, the Salvation Army erects "Angel Trees" in shopping malls. Each paper angel lists a child's given name, sex, age, identification number, clothing sizes, and a wish list. Shoppers choose an angel and place packages under the tree for that child.

My small hometown in Iowa has a similar program, called "Sharing Christmas." The weekly newspaper lists participating families by number only, along with their wish list, mostly basic items that many of us take for granted. Family #7 would like a grocery box and boy's thermal underwear, sizes ten and twelve. Family #23 woman needs a pair of overshoes, size eight, husband needs a sweatshirt, extra large, and warm work gloves. Family #30 needs baby formula, and flannel pajamas for girl, size four. One little girl wished for a hairbrush. Imagine a child not having a hairbrush. Some lists include the latest popular toy or game, but those requests read like an afterthought, as if it might be considered frivolous for a child from a needy family to wish for an expensive toy. Some requests opt for the food box.

The Sharing Christmas program and Angel Trees are reminders of my childhood. Like many families during the Depression and thereafter, we were monetarily poor. At Christmastime, we received a food box from the town's Community Chest.

By Christmas Eve afternoon, the house was dressed for the holiday. The fragrant pine tree in the parlor, propped in a bucket of wet sand, held homemade ornaments and strung popcorn. Lead icicles sparkled in the soft glow of blue, red, and green bulbs hidden in the branches. A worn cardboard crèche sat on a table (one of the three Magi was missing); a lighted plastic wreath hung lopsided in the kitchen window, its electrical cord dangling to the nearest socket. Strung corner to corner of the dining room ceiling were red and green construction-paper chains we kids had cut and pasted together. The heat from the room often loosened the chains and they had to be rehung time and again.

Ma bustled about the kitchen rolling piecrusts and making turkey stuffing from dry bread, onions, and sage.

short Lent who owe money to be paid at Easter." Benjamin Franklin

"When will the box come?" one of us periodically asked.

"It'll come when it comes," was her unsatisfying answer.

The clock ticked slowly. As the afternoon drew to a close, the sky became splashed with variegated colors bleeding together like a child's watercolor painting. Drying her hands on her apron, Ma walked to the window and called, "Santa spilled his buckets of paint."

We scurried from all directions, wondering aloud which of the many colors sprinkled across the horizon had been used for the toys Santa would bring. Had he finished painting before the buckets tipped over? Was this his way of showing us that he had finished his job, that all was ready for that flight from afar?

"When will Santa come?" a little brother asked.

"Not until you're asleep," Ma said.

"When will the grocery box come?"

"Before long." She went back to work and, sure enough, within minutes the delivery truck lumbered around the corner, its tire chains squeaking on packed snow.

The box was delivered by our neighbor, at whose grocery store some of the food was purchased. He and Ma visited for a moment, she thanked him, and they wished each other a Merry Christmas as he left.

~§~ "At Christmas play and make good cheer, for Christmas comes

We kids gathered around the table. From the box Ma pulled a plump turkey, a pound of butter (a glorious treat for oleomargarine users), a can of coffee, a jar of pimento olives, a can of jellied cranberry sauce, a fat clump of celery whose leafy top smelled as fresh as spring, several warty sweet potatoes, and cans of mincemeat and pumpkin that would become pie before Ma's workday ended.

"That's everything," she said, closing the lid. I knew that wasn't everything. In the bottom of the box were goodies for our stockings: ribboned candies, nuts in the shell, and fragrant oranges. Fresh fruit during Iowa's severe winters was expensive, so oranges were as welcome as St. Nick himself.

Today, reaching back to my Midwest roots, and in my parents' name, I contribute to the Sharing Christmas program in the small community that once nurtured my family. I do it for the kids who might be waiting at the window, wondering when the delivery will come.

And I pluck an angel from the Salvation Army's tree. My latest angel was Maria. I'll never meet Maria, but I know her; she's the child I used to be. I'll wager that Maria, and the scores of children whose names appear on the trees, will someday, in one way or another, sponsor angels of their own, in keeping with Christmas past.

Passover Memories

Suki Stone

Passover in my family was a busy time of the year – cleaning house, sprucing things up, washing the second set of dishes, and such. I had to dry all the dishes individually. It was a time of looking forward to change, as well as a time of looking back. My dad was in charge of us kids, making sure we all had jobs helping Mom get things ready for Passover time. The Haggadahs were out, and there was a special ceremony to reflect on the lives of relatives who had passed. We lit two special candles – one each for my mom's and dad's families – instead of lighting individual candles for each relative who had gone before.

I was put in charge of setting the table. My oldest brother Richard always made a sarcastic remark about being sure to set a special place for Elijah. After the conclusion of the Seder, there is a universally accepted custom of pouring a cup of wine, the "Cup of Elijah," then opening the front door of the home, and reciting several verses from the Psalms, wherein we beseech God to pour His wrath upon our persecutors and oppressors. At this moment, according to tradition, our homes are graced by the presence of Elijah the Prophet. Wide-eyed, I anticipated his arrival.

As a young girl, I also helped Mom prepare the food. We did not keep kosher, but my mom was conscious that we must have all the traditional components of Passover. She made sure the appropriate foods were on the Seder plate and that dad bought the Manischewitz wine, which was far too sweet even for a child.

My dad was always anxious to eat. Tradition, however, required that he must read for three hours from the Haggadah before we could start the meal. It was interactive: he would say the prayers, and we would have to respond to each prayer. He would have my oldest brother read the "four questions," even though they were meant to be read by the youngest child. Through the years, Dad began to skip over sections of the service, which short-ened the reading to about 45 minutes. By that time, my youngest brother, Robert, was able to read and respond to the four questions.

One year, while my dad was reading the Hagga-dah and explaining the meal portions on the Seder plate, our dog Stripe created a big commotion run-ning around under the table, which caused us all to push our chairs back. Suddenly, Stripe grabbed a corner of the table cloth in his teeth, and the Seder plate bounced to the floor, splattering in every direction. She grabbed the meat and ran toward the

centrate properly on blowing other people to pieces if their minds are

kitchen, with my mom trailing behind her shaking her napkin furiously.

"Richard! Get this dog outside! Hurry up!" Dad yelled. He was livid. Our Passover meal was interrupted, an unforgiveable act.

Robert said, "Wait. The dog only listens to me." He chased Stripe out the door and gave her a stern talk; he did not believe in corporal punishment.

Dad asked me to help Mom clean up the mess and re-prepare the Seder plate. We were forced to substitute left-over steak from yesterday's supper for the beautiful prime rib mother had lovingly prepared for the holiday.

The only consolation to this memorable Passover fiasco was that the service was cut very short. We got right to the four questions. We did not even bother to say them all. Everyone was famished by this point.

My dad always told a story at the beginning of the Passover meal. The same year as the Stripe fiasco, he told about a time when he was four or five years old and was called to Zaide's (grandfather in Yiddish) lap before the Seder meal. Zaide's purpose was to tell him where the Matzah was hidden. It was tradition that the youngest children were given a gift for finding the Matzah which had been hidden somewhere around the house. Dad said he believed that Zaide always wanted him to be the one to find it.

poisoned by thoughts suitable to the twenty-fifth of December."

One year, after we three kids were grown and on our own, Dad was called upon to substitute for the father of a very close Orthodox family friend at a Passover Meal. Although my dad had grown up in an Orthodox home, he and Mom had become Reformed Jews by this time. Assuming the role as head of that family, he was required to recite all prayers in Hebrew and was given other responsibilities for which he was not prepared. As he proceeded through the Seder, he stumbled often and was politely corrected by the host family. Dad felt embarrassed, but he managed to make it though the entire meal – which lasted six-and-one-half hours. Mom said he preferred not to accept any Passover Seder invitations after that. When they were invited back the following year, Dad was told he did not have to sit at the head of the table as the father substitute again. In that case, they accepted the invitation.

I have many memories of my dad's stories, my mom's perfect meals, and my happy moments growing up in a Jewish home. Passover was one of the family celebrations that brought us closer together. The event always reminded me of changes in each of our lives and changes we shared as a family.

Independence Day

President Franklin D. Roosevelt said, "In the truest sense, freedom cannot be bestowed; it must be achieved." The United States is a testimony to this adage – from the Revolutionary War to the present day. Many people mistakenly assume July 4th is the date that America won its independence from Great Britain. However, July 4, 1776, is actually the date the second Continental Congress adopted the Declaration of Independence, severing ties from the motherland. By the time Congress adopted the Declaration of Independence, the war was already being fought. A long and tedious battled ensued to determine the nation's fate. The Revolutionary War was the first truly "American" war, the first test of national unity and patriotism.

The new nation prevailed and set itself upon a course that would lead to world prominence. To guide it, representatives from all states assembled to hammer out a Constitution clearly delineating rights and responsibilities of its citizens. The Constitution is a living document, meaning that it can be amended. Therein lies the hope and strength of the nation for which patriots willingly gave their lives.

Traditions and icons include

- red, white, and blue decorations
- prominent displays of the American flag
- fireworks and firework displays
- local and national parades
- picnics, barbecues, and visits to parks

Color Me Pink

Marie Asner

When I was a child in elementary school, the favorite doll for girls was the bride doll, complete with long, white satin dress, white veil, white shoes and white bouquet. I wanted this doll very much. It seemed as though every girl had a vision of a wedding in a floor-length white gown, and it began with her own bride doll. In my small, rural town, girls in primary grades still wore inexpensive cotton dresses, sometimes decorated with buttons and bits of lace, while boys wore denim overalls knee-patched with any colorful fabric handy.

I was in the third grade and wanted that bride doll as a Christmas present. As soon as school started in September, I began writing to Santa Claus. Not only did I write a weekly letter and give it to my parents to mail, but I also told every girl in my class that Santa would bring me a bride doll – but then every girl told every other girl the same thing. All the girls wanted one.

Halloween went by, then Thanksgiving and finally the Christmas holidays began. By this time, I had written sixteen letters to Santa Claus with the

about the spark of the divine in all of us made in God's image."

same request: a bride doll. By the second week in December, our live tree was up in a pail of water, fully decorated and the lights strung. The only thing left was a certain package to go under that tree.

On Christmas Eve, it was traditional to go to evening church, then home to open presents. Santa Claus always made early rounds in this town. That evening, my mother was delayed a few minutes and caught up with Dad and me by the church door. We lived a block from the church and walked slowly. I could barely sit through the Children's Service and hoped we could sing our carols faster so I could go home to my bride doll. At the final Amen, I squirmed my way through the maze of well-dressed children, found my parents and ran home ahead of them. No one locked doors in this town, so I opened the front door and ran in, and there under the tree was a doll...a bride doll... dressed in PINK? Pink satin shoes, pink satin dress with pink net over the skirt, a pink satin circle on her head with a pink net veil – and she was holding a bouquet of pink flowers. I was stunned.

Who ever heard of a pink bride doll? Don't brides always wear white? What was I going to tell the girls at school? I could barely touch the doll. Later, softly crying, I put the doll in my clothes closet. Dad complained about "...spoiled children today..." and headed for a glass of wine, while my Mother looked sad. I didn't take the doll out of the closet once. Those Christmas holidays went on forever. I avoided the usual winter sports like skating or skiing with friends, preferring to go alone. In fact, I didn't even want to go back to school in January and face my friends.

The New Year came and then the first day of school. We were supposed to bring a special holiday present as a "Show and Tell." I pleaded ill that day, but my mother knew better, made me get dressed and sent me to school. I went empty-handed, telling my teacher I forgot my present. I was the only girl who forgot a present, but there were boys who forgot, too. They had wanted new sleds or skis or skates and didn't get them. It was of little comfort. They didn't have to worry about the color pink.

Then, it happened. The wealthiest girl in class got up and showed a bride doll wearing white. It had a white satin gown with flowing satin train, little satin cap with pearls and a net veil, satin shoes trimmed with pearl buttons and white paper flowers stuck to one hand. I was close to tears as she proudly showed the doll to everyone. It was magnificent. Then, she turned to me and said with a teasing look, "Where is your doll? I heard she was dressed in pink." I was horrified and my face turned red…who else knew? I hadn't told anyone.

My teacher smiled and said, "Didn't you know? Pink is the spring fashion color in Paris this year."

Paris? My pink doll was in fashion? Just before tears were ready to slide down my cheeks, other girls started to whisper. "My sister always wanted a pink dress...wherever did your Mom get one?... she must have gone to the big city for it...how could you forget to bring it...?"

Suddenly, my absent doll was the hit of the classroom. I ran home after school, skipped through the house to my closet and brought out the pink bride doll. I couldn't wait for the next day so I could take her to school and a place of honor near my desk. I hadn't noticed before, but she looked rather good in pink. It was her color.

A few weeks later, I found out that there was a shortage of white taffeta, satin, tulle and net to be had for any special dress. Whatever color of fine fabric anyone found was deemed good enough for a special occasion dress. Pink was now THE color. One of the girls in my class whispered that the wealthy girl's grandmother had made her bride doll's dress from an old petticoat.

I learned that it isn't the gift that counts but the giver and what goes on behind the gift to make it happen. I found out that my mother knew my teacher was getting married that summer and that the teacher's mother was making the bridesmaid's dresses out of pink fabric. My mother had gotten the scraps of material and made my bride doll's gown. My teacher had known all along that I was getting a pink bride doll. I lived in a town of many secrets, but after that, one thing was well-known – that the pink bride doll was a cherished item in my home.

Once Upon an Easter

Elizabeth Howard

Fire stoked in the potbelly stove,
the country church warms up
quickly this Easter morning.
As I stand to read the Scripture
for the Sunday school lesson,
a wasp rouses in the rafters
and flies about drunkenly.
It settles on my hand and dozes,
antennae quivering. Knowing
the children will panic if they
see the wasp, I read on, one eye
on the wasp, one on the filmy page.
The reading finished, the organ
erupts in an arpeggio.
The wasp rises, one of the halo
of wasps circling the golden light
spilling in the window.
I join the chorus of voices,
singing "Alleluia, Amen."

Labor Day Lament

Joanne Faries

huddled on beach towels
hands clasped around knees
steady winds blow
fine sandblast

wiggle toes in sand
determined to
bid summer farewell
hang with friends
discuss fall plans

lower sky meets
gray-green waves
pounding surf
taunts boogie-board-
toting bathers as
lifeguards whistle
riptide warnings

resigned

we celebrate summer's
last hurrah

Labor Day

Labor Day is celebrated on the first Monday in September in the United States. At least two stories are put forth as to the origin of Labor Day as a celebration. One involves Matthew Maguire, a New York machinist and secretary of the Central Labor Union, who proposed that a date be set aside to honor workers. Also in 1882, Peter J. McGuire of the American Federation of Labor, is said to have proposed the same suggestion after observing an annual labor celebration in Toronto, Canada. However, Oregon was the first state to make it a holiday, in 1887.

In the 1880s, American laborers were commonly forced to work twelve-hour days. The first major Labor Day rally was in 1882, demanding, among other things, eight-hour workdays. The Pullman Strike of 1894 involving some 250,000 workers in 27 states resulted in the deaths of many U.S. military and U.S. Marshals. President Grover Cleveland stepped in to reconcile matters, urging

Congress to rush through legislation making Labor Day a national holiday – in recognition of the contributions of workers to national well-being. At least thirty states officially celebrated Labor Day by the time it became a federal holiday in 1894.

Today, the federal holiday honors some 154.4 million American workers, of whom nearly 83% receive health benefits.

Traditions and icons include

- annual observance on the first Monday of September
- full holiday pay in honor of American workers
- family gatherings and celebrations

Zola's Flowers

Mary Chandler

In early March, Zola mulched the rich Idaho soil in her flower garden in preparation for spring planting. She smiled as she felt the moist soil beneath her fingers. Planting new bulbs beside her other perennials and dropping Ferry-Morse bachelor's button, zinnia, and buttercup seeds into the earth brought memories of past Memorial Days. She could hardly wait to share her flowers at the annual family gathering in the Weiser, Idaho, cemetery.

As the sun warmed the earth, Zola watered and tended her flowers. Soon tulips and daffodils danced in the breeze; regal irises welcomed her; and the sight of lavender, purple, and white peonies – her favorites – gladdened her heart.

Zola's flowers offered her a respite from the long, hard days on the fifty-two-acre farm she shared with her husband Paul and their four young children. What with milking, tending to the chickens, working in the fields, and caring for her family, the days sometimes seemed endless. She looked forward to enjoying the Memorial Day reunion and

'Tis the season for kindling the fire of hospitality in the hall, the genial

picnic and seeing the beauty of her flowers on the graves.

Before World War II, phones were scarce in the country, and most farm families traveled only when necessary. Zola, a gregarious soul, had grown up in Salt Lake City, and she missed her family. Neighboring farmers got together to harvest crops and to help one another, and there were taffy pulls, popcorn, and homemade doughnuts for the sing-alongs, dances, and card games on Saturday nights – but it just wasn't the same. Except for rare visits from her two sisters, Zola saw little of her own family. *Luckily*, she thought, *Paul's relatives treat me as one of their own.*

The extended Chandler family had all settled in the same general area, close enough to gather each Memorial Day. This holiday was their annual chance to visit with all of their relatives. Hearing about the early pioneers always fascinated Zola, and she eagerly awaited the yearly get-togethers, when four generations of the living gathered to renew ties and revere the dead.

When Memorial Day finally arrived, Zola could slip outside and cut her flowers. But first, she had to help with the milking, prepare mush, eggs and toast for breakfast, and make the baked beans and potato salad for the picnic. As she snipped lilac blooms, yellow and red roses, daisies, pansies, peonies, and all the rest, she thought about the reunion.

Soon buckets of cut flowers completely filled the bed of the pickup truck. The freshly-scrubbed faces of the four Chandler children peeked through the blooms. As it bounced along the road on the way to the cemetery, the yellow International pickup – with its shiny black fenders – looked like a giant bumblebee.

"Hop out, kids," Paul said, once the family had reached their destination. He grinned, hitched up his overalls, and scooped up five-year-old Margie.

The children hurried across the grass to play with their cousins.

"Come play horseshoes," Paul's brother Kenelm hollered.

"Need more help?" Paul asked his wife after they had unloaded the flower buckets from the truck bed.

"No, thanks," Zola answered. "You go ahead, and I'll join you later."

One by one, Zola selected flowers from her many buckets and created bouquets to place on the waiting graves. Her eyes filled with tears as she read some of the headstones. *Paul and I are so blessed,* she thought. *All our children lived.* The headstones reminded her that in most families, one or more children died young, victims of diphtheria, whooping cough, measles, or pneumonia. Only empty hearts and faded numbers engraved in the granite stone – and sometimes a small faded photograph – remained to remind parents of a life that might have been. These losses touched Zola deeply. She honored each child who had died with a single rosebud.

Zola covered forgotten and neglected graves with flowers, too. Soldiers killed in the First World War, farmers and farm wives who had been victims of accidents, folks who had passed away from old age – all received the love and respect they deserved on this day of remembrance.

Aunt Fanny greeted Zola, wrapping her arms around Zola's neck. "We knew you were here," she said. "From up on the hill, we could see the usual big splotch of flowers where you'd been."

Zola looked over the graves and watched the remaining relatives and friends gathering. "Fanny," she said, "whole generations of what was, is, and might have been are all here, on this one spot."

Fanny nodded.

Zola placed a bunch of peonies on Grandpa Chandler's grave. "We just want you to know that it's so nice to be with you today," she whispered. She reached into her pocket for her handkerchief and wiped her eyes. "You're a real part of our reunion, you know – you, Grandma, and all the others who have gone on before."

Later, after tending the remaining graves, Zola and Paul spread their picnic blanket in the shade of a giant elm. The families shared food and stories of the people honored on this special day. The conversation continued throughout the afternoon and into the early evening. Zola knew that, like her, no one wanted to leave. Unless someone married or the family lost a loved one, this would be the only get-together for the whole clan until the next Memorial Day.

Finally, as daylight turned to dusk, Zola gathered her children together for a final walk through the cemetery.

When families read, work, and play by lantern after dark because they can't afford hookups to power lines – even though they're available, she thought, *when crops fail, and when lonesome folks do what they can to be less lonely, I have my flowers.* Her seven-year-old son, Don, leaned over to smell a yellow rose. Zola rumpled his hair and smiled. *And a wonderful family of my own.*

Cinco de Mayo

Carrie McClure

colorful sombreros tip forward
over smiling faces

swirling rainbow skirts
join in joy

all dancing, jumping
twirling in celebration

sweet drinks, soft pastries
tasty meats, delectable delights

share table tops
with red balloons and party favors

vibrant *mariachi* melodies
strong music and laughter fill the streets

on *cinco de mayo*
everyone is free

Love to Jim
Yes, I really did this!
Beth
Happy birthday

The "To Do" List

Beth Lynn Clegg

With Christmas just a week away, the antici-pation of celebrating this sacred holiday was building. Parties with friends had been delightful. Our church choir and minister had lifted my spirits. Cards had been mailed. Cookies were in the freezer. Gifts for others were under my small artificial tree. The lunch menu at my daughter-in-law and son's home was set, and I'd selected a dish to prepare. A bit hectic, yes, but that's to be expected this time of year. Yet something was missing.

I scanned my "to do" list. My news carrier, hair-stylist, and mailman were taken care of, plus the latter two had received cookies. The garbage men were missing. Wait. Let me explain.

After reading an article several years ago about remembering service providers we take for granted, I liked the idea, and it had become a holiday tradition. Tomorrow was the last trash pickup before the holiday. Cash and cookies were on the kitchen counter when I retired. Next morning, sounds from the garbage truck and my alarm clock blended. By

Avarice is in its prime, / Yet feed the Poor at Christmas time." Poor

the time I got outside, the truck was six townhouses past mine, but this had become a mission. I would not be denied.

Remember those commercials where couples dash toward one another across lush alpine meadows, their filmy garments and hair flowing in the breeze? Well, think alley, overturned trash containers, a faded nightshirt with a black and white cat stretching from the shoulder to a hem beginning to sag, boobs and floral slides flapping in sync, as I ran waving cash and a bag of garbage in one hand, and a bag of cookies in the other.

The truck stopped. The driver leapt down, shouting words I couldn't hear as we raced toward one another. Suddenly, I was in a crushing embrace. As soft lips brushed my cheek, he said, "Merry Christmas. Merry, merry Christmas. *Gracias*. Thank you, *Señora. Gracias.*"

Dark wavy hair topped his youthful face set with pitch-black eyes now dancing with delight. The tremor in his broken English left little doubt that he'd never been remembered. It became difficult to speak, but thankfully my voice didn't fail me. "I wish it could've been more, *Señor*. Merry Christmas."

Every move was recorded by our 24/7 neighborhood security cameras. Whoever viewed it might've been as shocked as I was. If so, so be it. In a most unlikely way, I'd rediscovered the true meaning of Christmas.

Halloween

Halloween is celebrated on October 31st annually. From traditions of the early Christian churches, it is also known as "All Hallows Eve" or "All Saints Day." The traditions of Halloween trace their origins to the Celts of the United Kingdom over 2,000 years ago. Religious leaders, called "Druids," celebrated the feast of "Samhain" on November 1st each year. They believed that the night before the feast was very special – a night when spirits of the dead could walk the earth in search of the homes where they spent their mortal lives. The Celts wore costumes and scary attire to ward off any malevolent spirits.

With the coming of Roman Christianity, even deep-rooted Celtic traditions in the United Kingdom underwent some change. Pope Gregory IV sought harmony between the Celtic traditions of Samhain and those of All Saints Day. Hence, there arose hybrid celebrations and traditions that have made their way through time to present-day conceptions of Halloween. In fact, "Hallowe'en" is the shortening over time of "All Hallows

Christian holidays that move in sync, like the ice skating pairs we saw

Eve," traditionally observed on October 31st by Christians.

By the mid-1800s, Irish immigrants to America brought with them Celtic and Halloween traditions which spread quickly to other cultures. The tradition of trick-or-treating, for example, also has Celtic origins. At harvest time, people would go about asking for offerings of food to sacrifice to the gods, a way of honoring them for the harvest. The practice eventually evolved into the modern practice of asking for candy and treats.

Traditions and icons include

- scary creatures: spiders, ghouls, hobgoblins, witches, etc.
- hayrides and parties
- bonfires and scary stories
- wearing of masks and costumes
- carving pumpkins into jack-o-lanterns
- trick-or-treating

A Small Christmas Box

The Rev. Dr. Bill Olewiler

I had wanted a dog for a long time. And year by year, birthday by birthday, Christmas by Christmas, I did not get a dog. Momma would not have one in the house – even though she had grown up in a household filled with dogs.

Christmas 1955 arrived; I had just turned ten. Under the tree were big boxes, little boxes, medium-sized boxes. Out of them came clothes (yuck), plastic models, new cars for my electric train, candy. Sitting alone under the tree was the smallest box, neatly wrapped but too tiny to hold anything interesting. I finally picked it up and opened it.

Out fell a red plastic dog collar, puppy-sized.

Dad and Momma explained that the collar would fit a newborn Dachshund puppy, still not weaned, still too small to leave its mother. But this would be my dog, the answer to my dreams.

Fritz and I were companions for another twelve years, until he died.

July 4

Plano, Texas

Becky Haigler

By thousands we stream into the park
to stake out little homesteads with quilts
and camp chairs made in China. Pakistani
teenagers play touch football, not soccer.
A Mexican family eats take-out pizza.
Women in saris stroll past Mohawked
youth in black and chains. Plano's
finest bicycle patrol weaves around
baby strollers. Children make patterns
of cold fire with tubes of chemical light.
At last, the sky blooms in showering color.
Groups look away from themselves
to the call of unthreatening thunder;
"bombs bursting in air" without menace.
We have gathered – red and yellow,
black and white – on this greensward
without the inconvenient walls of life,
to celebrate. We are Americans.

Dad's Special Gift

Mary Chandler

Dad anchored the wooden stand to our ceiling-high Christmas tree as it lay on the living room floor – while his five children, ornaments in hand, cheered him on.

"That should do it," he said, jostling the stand to make sure it didn't wiggle.

Grabbing the center of the trunk, he pulled and shoved until the enormous tree stood upright in the far corner of the room. Whistling "Deck the Halls," he strung the lights. Then, hoisting his hefty frame onto a chair, he topped the tree with a beautiful fluffy-haired angel whose lopsided halo made me smile.

"We need a new angel," my brother Clifford said. "Her wings look like a glider ready to take off."

"Shh," I whispered. With wartime shortages in 1944, I knew that one didn't replace angels or much of anything else on a whim.

Most of our neighbors selected trees from Anderson's Christmas tree lot, but Dad borrowed Mr. Tatton's truck, hiked up the cold, snowy mountainside, and cut our tree himself – his Christmas gift to his children.

Soon we were busy hanging hand-made ornaments, making popcorn chains, and smoothing out each tinfoil icicle before carefully placing it onto that huge tree. The tree glimmered and glistened.

My sixteen-month-old brother Stan pointed at his reflection in a shiny red ornament. "Baby," he said, giggling and pressing his nose against the glowing ball.

Dad chuckled, bent down, and kissed Stan's cheek. I could almost feel Dad's soft mustache against my own skin. I smiled and sat on the sofa, awaiting Dad's annual reading of the Christmas story, a Christmas Eve tradition in our home.

I was nine-and-a-half years old. For weeks and weeks my brothers Charley, eleven, and Clifford, seven, and I had been saving every penny we could earn and find. The three of us had raked leaves, shoveled snow, delivered newspapers, babysat, and even searched the fairground after the carnival left town for change that might have been dropped. Dad didn't know it, but we, along with our mother, had a plan.

"What would you like for Christmas?" Dad had asked when he saw us leafing through our Sears-Roebuck Christmas "wish book."

Mama smiled and winked. I winked back.

"I'd like a doctor kit," Charley and Clifford answered.

"Me, too!" I said.

Dad's eyebrows curled up over his glasses, and his hazel eyes looked at each of us in turn. "You got those last year," he said. "Wouldn't you like something different?"

My brothers and I exchanged knowing looks and shook our heads. We knew that a fat Christmas stocking crammed with candy and nuts, a tart red apple in the toe, and a juicy orange plugging the heel would await each of us on Christmas morning. We also knew that the sibling who had drawn our name would surprise us with a yo-yo, a box of watercolors, or a treasured book from the library rummage sale. Besides, with our doctor kits we could give each other pretend shots, listen to heartbeats with the plastic stethoscope, and ration out those miniature multi-colored candy pills so they would last until Easter. Most important, we knew that our parents could afford what we'd chosen.

Mama taught fifth grade; Dad was the principal of her school and two others. Eighteen years older than my mother – who was more relaxed – Dad was from what he liked to call "the old school." Translated, that meant that he periodically administered standardized tests to all the students in his three schools to monitor their scholastic progress, and he personally checked each response with an answer key, red pencil in hand.

Correcting the tests he didn't mind, but administering them rankled his soul. A few weeks earlier when he'd come to administer the tests in my classroom, I'd watched as he'd waited until the second hand of the classroom clock was straight up. He then uttered those frightening words, "YOU MAY NOW BEGIN" – and then later, "STOP!" Each test contained several sections, all of them timed. Dad did a lot of clock watching. That's when I got the Christmas idea.

Every evening before we went to bed, Charley, Clifford, and I counted the money we had saved.

"I must send the order off tomorrow," Mama told us ten days before Christmas, "to make sure it gets here on time."

We needed three more dollars.

"Let's sell homemade Christmas candy," I suggested.

"What about vinegar taffy?" Clifford said. "We can color one batch red and the other batch green."

Mama nodded. "Good idea. I'll help you."

Charley measured the sugar, water, butter, and vinegar and set it on the stove to boil. The kitchen smelled worse than when Mama poured the vinegar rinse over my head after she washed my hair. When the mixture finally boiled down, Mama dropped a little into some cold water.

"It's done!" she said. "See the firm ball?" She poured the candy into pie tins to cool and added the food coloring.

We buttered our hands and pulled, stretched, and twisted until the taffy changed texture. Quickly, we laid the taffy ropes onto waxed paper covered with powdered sugar. Grabbing her long kitchen scissors, Mama cut the taffy into bite-sized pieces.

"Bundle up," she said, as we prepared to go door-to-door peddling our ribbon candy throughout the neighborhood. "It's cold out there."

"You take this side of the street, Charley. Clifford and I will take the other side."

For an hour we trudged through the snow, knocking on doors, usually hearing "No, thank you," and occasionally selling a few pieces of taffy. My hands felt like icicles. So did my toes.

"This candy's probably frozen solid," Charley said. "I know I am."

Clifford blew on his hands. "Me, too. Can we go home?"

I gave him one of my looks. "Let's try the next block."

As we climbed the steep hill, the wind whistled through our coats and rattled icy tree branches in the tall oaks. At the top of the hill, music poured from Dr. Whiting's house on the corner. A blazing fire shone through the picture window, and people filled the living room.

"Let's skip this house," Charley said. "They're having a Christmas party."

Too late; Mrs. Whiting must have spotted us. The door opened wide, and a tall woman with a kind face smiled at three half-frozen children.

"Would you li-i-ke to buy some Chris-s-s-tmas taffy?" Clifford asked, his teeth chattering.

"I believe I would," she said. Without asking the price, she took the remaining candy and, after a few words with her husband, slipped three dollars into Clifford's coat pocket.

Sliding down that hill towards home, our feet scarcely touched the ground.

Now, it was Christmas Eve. Wood crackled in the fireplace, and a warm glow filled the room. The rest of the family joined me on the sofa, where we sat gazing at our newly decorated tree with the slightly bedraggled angel at its crown.

"It's time for the Christmas Story," Dad said.

He opened the family Bible and began to read the familiar story of the birth of the Christ Child, while Mama, her brown eyes shining, cradled her own little son in her arms.

When the story ended, we gathered around our ancient upright piano. Charley played the piano, and we sang all three verses of my favorite carol, "Silent Night." I thought about Mary, Joseph, and the baby Jesus. I thought, too, about the shepherds in the fields and the wise men who journeyed from

which makes us fathers and sons." Johann Schiller ~§~ "Our Lord has

afar, bringing gifts to share with the Holy Child. As I sang, the spirit of Christmas surrounded me, filling my heart, touching my soul.

Later, as I lay in my bed upstairs, I thought about another gift – the special one.

"It's wrapped and hidden in the tree," Mama whispered, tucking my covers around me and kissing my cheek. "I'll tell the boys."

When Christmas morning dawned, we lined up from youngest to oldest in the hallway downstairs. We couldn't go into the living room – at least not yet. First, Dad had to peek into that room, turn on the tree lights, and announce in his booming voice, "Old St. Nick has been here!"

We waited, but, happily, not for long. Eyes aglow, we scampered into the living room. Gaily wrapped gifts awaited us, and our stockings were right there where they always were on Christmas Day, filled to the brim with candy and nuts and hanging like colorful rag dolls over the back of the sofa.

With our stockings, we settled down on a spot on the floor, where we could store the surprises that awaited us. Mother handed Dad the presents, one at a time. Dad read the tag and announced:"To Mary, from Santa," or "To Charley, from Kaye," until all the gifts had found a home.

Only one child opened his gifts at a time, beginning with the youngest. The rest of us savored that person's joy and excitement. I helped my little brother Stan.

Dad, being the oldest, always opened his presents last. This Christmas brought him the usual array of grown-up necessities: a pair of stockings, a large eraser for his schoolwork, three red pencils, and a small collapsible leather coin purse. He received each gift with an expansive grin and a heartfelt, "Thank you."

"Well," Dad announced, when nothing but discarded wrapping paper adorned the worn carpet, "we've had a wonderful Christmas!"

"Wait a minute," Mama said. "I think I see another gift."

Reaching back into the branches of that sweet-smelling pine tree, she drew out a small package wrapped in gold and tied with tinsel. "To Dad," she announced, handing the gift to him.

Dad slowly unwrapped the box and looked inside. A long sigh finally broke the stillness. Tears spilled down my father's cheeks as he held his eighteen-dollar stopwatch by its golden chain so that we could admire his treasure. Then he opened the case, and, in a quivering voice, read the inscription: "To Dad, with our love." His eyes were not the only ones filled with tears.

Time has tucked away many years since then, and many Christmases have come and gone, but the Christmas of Dad's special gift will always be my favorite.

Veterans Day

Veterans Day is a federal holiday set aside to honor both living and dead members of the military in times of both war and peace. November 11th commemorates the end of World War I in 1918. President Woodrow Wilson proclaimed the date, originally known as "Armistice Day," as a time to celebrate World War I soldiers. But it wasn't until 1938 that Armistice Day was declared a federal holiday by Congress. World War I was dubbed "The War to End All Wars." By the end of World War II, it was apparent that the name Armistice Day needed to be replaced by a more general term, so as to include American veterans of all wars – past and future. Hence, in 1954 the holiday was officially known as Veterans Day.

For reasons having greatly to do with family, Congress passed the "Uniform Monday Holiday Act" in 1968, which changed the traditional dates of several holidays. Veterans Day was moved from November 11th to the fourth Monday of October. In the wake of great protest, federal legislation restored the original date, where it remains today.

Traditions and icons

- family gatherings and picnics
- prominent displays of American flags
- local and national parades and ceremonies
- decorating the gravesites of fallen soldiers

Brown Bags and Christmas Paper

Dixon Hearne

On the outskirts of West Monroe, Louisiana, fireworks were perfectly legal in the 1950s – even encouraged. What better time to celebrate than Christmas Eve? Mimmaw and Papaw Simpkins lived in a frame house that Papaw and his brothers built by themselves on the edge of town. Every Christmas Eve, the extended family – aunts, uncles, cousins – gathered there for an evening of joy and gift-giving. We kids could care less about the socks and shirts and underwear under the tree – at least, for a while. We came each year with bigger thoughts in mind – fireworks!

We were each given a brown paper bag from Gentry's Grocery weighted down with sparklers and brightly-colored packets of one- and two-inch firecrackers – more than we could ever hope to pop in a night. We'd been taught how to carefully light and release them, and the older kids helped the younger ones, just to be safe.

In no time, the air was electric with hissing sparklers dancing in the dark, red and orange flashes followed by reverberating pows and cracks and fizzles. There was no yelling or complaining from neighbors – every kid on the block joined in the celebration. It was the most exciting night of the year. But we were not thinking of the Baby Jesus or even Santa Claus at the time. We were pirates and cowboys and army soldiers bombing our way to victory. And win, we did. That is, until that one particular Christmas threatened to become our last great crusade.

"Move back!" Frankie yelled, his arm cocked to lob a lit two-incher. Mitzi, always the excitable one, clutched her bag and froze. "Run!" Frankie screamed, his lob a serious miss-toss. "It's lit somewhere!"

We all scurried toward the house – all except Mitzi, who remained planted in place, stiff with panic.

"Run, Mitzi!" we all pleaded. "Run for your life!"

It had passed the time for the two-incher to explode, and we all knew it. Darla gasped and flew to rescue Mitzi. But before she had covered half the distance, Darla's paper bag commenced dancing to sounds like popcorn in a kettle. The fireworks sprang to life in a spangle of brilliant flashes and bangs that literally hopped and hurled and burst their way to freedom – a paralyzing sight. We stared in awe as Darla, still clutching the remnants of her ragged bag, danced a joker's jig amidst the snapping creatures that held her hostage. Mitzi

philosophers." Harriet Beecher Stowe ~§~ "Extremism in the defense

tuned up and bawled, and the rest of us fell down from fright or belly laughter.

"That could have put my eye out!" Darla said. "I could have lost a hand or foot!" She was red-hot angry that we didn't try to help her. But we had no idea what to do, it happened so fast – and it had never happened before.

Inside the house, our parents, aunts, and uncles – lost to their own merriment – were unaware of the excitement out back. We were now ready for a cup of cocoa and the gift exchange.

There would be eggnog and sweet potato pie – pecan for those who wished – and hugs all around. And we'd soon begin the yearly ritual of deciding who would pass out the gifts, replete with tedious argument over whose turn it was, and why. The grown-ups told us not to fight over it, then left us to our wrangling.

Darla argued that she should be the gift-giver because she was the eldest girl (and the victim of a recent, though unmentionable, life-changing experience), but my brother Ryan reminded her that he was the first-born grandchild and therefore the true elder. Darren and Cindy moaned the plight of middle children, who got squeezed out and suffered in a thousand ways. The youngest had no chance – ever! No matter how we begged and pleaded, the job was always either too big or not our turn.

Papaw settled the matter. He picked a number between one and twenty-five. No matter who won, though, it would be called unfair. There would be no pleasing sour losers – all except my cousin Becky and me. We had no real feelings on the matter, since it was already predetermined that we didn't count. Our bounty under the tree would make its way to us soon enough. In the meantime, while they pushed and shoved and argued, Becky and I prostrated ourselves before the tree dreaming and play-guessing what each secret package held.

Shirt boxes were deceptive – they held almost everything. Tiny boxes were perplexing. In years past, they'd held rings, watches, bracelets, neck-laces – even folding money. Awkward packages seemed the easiest, if we could sneak a feel. The basketball and hoop were too easy, the baton a cinch. By the time Papaw named the winner, we had already made a mental list of everyone's gift and watched with great anticipation for each one to emerge from its Christmas wrapping.

Darla won as gift-giver this year and dove right in. Talk-talk-talk – so much we could barely hear our names being called. No one stayed in place but moved excitedly about, sharing their good fortune. And – right on cue – Gene Autry belted out "Here Comes Santa Claus," something Becky and I alone seemed to notice. Eyes popped wide, and smiles and laughter filled the room, enough joy to carry us another entire year. Of course, the downside of being gift-giver was that you were the last one to see your own loot. Just like the Bible says: first shall be last.

The parlor was a veritable heap of knick-knacks and doodads and clothing of every imaginable shape, size, and color. The candles on the mantel and the shimmering tree brought a warm holiday glow to the room. At length our attention was diverted by an all-too-familiar voice from the Victrola – Bing Crosby crooning "White Christmas." No one told us kids to shush – we just did. And the holiday spirit lingered with us late into the evening and all the way home.

On balance, that Christmas Eve was not so different from all the former ones, except that Becky and I became better gift-guessers than before. My family, like so many families around the world, continued to hold tight to our traditions. We gathered close to my grandparents' hearth at Christmastime, until each of us cousins had our own hearths to draw our families near, creating new memories that linked us together across time.

Resolute

Barbara B. Rollins

I resolve to make no resolution,
to avoid disgrace of failure
when the year's a few weeks old.
Lose weight, keep a clean house,
gossip less, enjoy more – oh, yes,
I yearn for these. Five hundred miles run
a few at a time; piles of worthy books
made mine, internalized; to be a person I admire
when ads on billboards again entreat
a list of goals – buy here, use this...
Yes, I'll tackle these, my heart's desire,
but just for now, only today,
repeated day by day
as calendar pages expire.

The Christmas Sweater

Marilyn E. Freeman

I have wonderful memories of Christmas 1962. I was a new bride of one month. We didn't have much but as they say – love conquers all. If that were true, we could have done anything. We were both teenagers and sure that we would have a lasting, 'til-death-do-us-part marriage.

We didn't have much money, but we both worked; he brought home forty-two dollars a week and I brought home twenty-four. We lived in a one-bedroom apartment that was an addition to the back of a house. Our rent was fifty dollars a month. We had a dog – named Grumpy. Life was good, and we were happy. I know our parents didn't think we would survive, but they never let on about their fears.

Christmas was just around the corner and I had to buy a few presents. The most important one would be for my new husband. I was a little short on cash so I had to shop really carefully. I found the perfect white sweater. The front had buttons and pockets. This was just his style. My only problem was the price – $19.98. That's about what I had to buy all my gifts that year. I couldn't spend that much money on one gift. I asked one of the sales ladies if she had anything similar that cost less. She told me that sweater was on sale, fifty percent off. Wow, I couldn't believe my ears. I could spend $9.98 and try to make it up some other way. Maybe I could work a few overtime hours.

The next day, my mom and I went to a little shopping center. Everywhere we went they had Christmas trees and decorations for sale. My mom asked if I was going to buy a tree. I didn't want to tell her I really didn't have the money. I told her we would look at them on the weekend. I think she knew money was tight. She asked if she could buy us our first Christmas tree as a gift. I was so happy at that suggestion. We bought the perfect tree for a dollar fifty. Then she wanted to look at decorations. I tried to discourage her, but she was very determined to get some. As she was looking at decorations, I found a tree topper I loved. It was a plastic Santa face with cotton and tin foil trimming. It was adorable, and I had to have it for our first tree. The price was twenty-five cents. I insisted on paying for the Santa.

I couldn't wait for Christmas Eve to see the look on my husband's face when he opened his gift from me. He loved the sweater. We kept the Santa tree topper and used it every year for at least thirty years. It started getting frayed and ragged. We didn't throw it away; we wrapped it in tissue and

~8~ "The older I get, the smarter my father seems to get." Tim Russert kept it with our other decorations. Each year we looked at it and remembered our first Christmas.

He kept the sweater in his closet. That was almost fifty years ago. Over the years the sweater no longer fit him, but he kept it in his closet and wouldn't get rid of it. My husband passed away last year, just a few days short of our being married forty-nine years. Even though I gave away most of his clothes and things, I kept the sweater.

We did okay over the years. My husband was a very good provider and always took care of his family. As it turned out, as teens, we were right. We did have a 'til-death-do-you-part marriage.

And Still It Waves

Dixon Hearne

A sky ablaze
with exploding novas
and brilliant contrails
o'er ramparts streaming
struck a chord
in the heart of Key,
who paused in awe
to pen an anthem.

An Arbor Day

Becky Haigler

Twenty summers old,
five winters dead,
and rotten at the roots:
easily we down the oak.
Termites feast on its decay.

Dead before we came,
the wood is brittle, brittle.
Even large branches snap
easily under our heels.
The pile of kindling grows.

You pace the yard
to calculate a spot
for the apple tree we chose.
We liked its sturdy trunk,
no matter the crooked places.

We settle the new tree
strong and steady,
brick and mulch a circle.
How shall we care for the apple?
How make the fruit sweet?

He Took Me Fishing

Harvey Silverman

Father's Day. A day to celebrate dad. To honor him, to appreciate him, to love him. But I need no reminder.

As I told you, my mom got sick recently with a pulmonary infection and needed hospitalization. I also told you my dad has gotten rather frail physically, and has become more easily confused. It is a sad thing to watch. He was a very bright fellow, independent in thought, strong opinions, determined in life. That has all gradually left him.

With my mom's admission to the hospital, my brother and I knew that our dad couldn't be left home alone at night, so we took turns staying with him. We might leave him alone for a couple of hours in the daytime, but as the sun started to go down, he would get more confused and needed somebody to be there.

I drove an hour and a half after work to be with him. I'd try to visit my mom if time allowed and then go to their house to stay with my dad. He did not feel up to going to the hospital to visit her. As I drove to be there, my thoughts were about my folks, pondering life and getting old. I thought about my dad, about the fellow he used to be and the kind of dad he was.

My dad was a wonderful father. He laughed, he loved, he set examples.

He used to work twelve hours a day – six days a week in his drugstore for several years. I recall the big deal it was when, I suppose I was seven or eight, he was finally able to afford to hire a pharmacist to take care of things so he could have a half day off.

Despite so much time in his store working to support us, he still found time to do things with me. One thing we did, beginning when I was four, was to go fishing on his day off on Sunday. We were not at all very serious fishermen. I usually fished for bluegills or perch with worms for bait. My dad would fish often with shiners or sometimes lures for bass or pickerel. He also spent a lot of time patiently fixing my tangles. So, I thought a lot about him taking me fishing over the years.

He did other stuff with me, things I thought about. He cheered my mediocre athletic efforts. He would take me and my mom to Boston to watch the Red Sox play, back when you could buy a ticket on game day. When I was fourteen and again when I was fifteen, I got him to drive me and a few friends to New York to watch the Giants play football at Yankee Stadium. I would organize the guys in the early spring and we ordered the tickets. He drove us down, we all went to the game and then he drove us home, four hours each way, all in a day.

One winter when I was, I think, fifteen, I convinced him that we should build a sailfish – a twelve-foot sailing craft that you sit on, not in. We spent all winter in the basement building it and when spring came we just by the narrowest margin were able to get it out the door.

Those were the sorts of things I thought about. I was able to distill all the memories I had of my dad doing things with me, as well as the general job he did rearing me and the loving way we related after I became an adult to a simple statement: "He took me fishing."

Well, there I am, taking care of my dad, with my mom in the hospital. There is nobody to sort of "cover" for him, and I am there in the evening and night, when it is tougher for him. It has become clear to me that my dad is a lot worse than I thought. He is much more confused than I had cause to realize. It is all upsetting for me. I have said before that this frail, confused old man is not really my dad, not much anyhow. It is even more clear now.

It is late night. I have finally gotten my dad settled in bed. I wait to be certain he does not get up and begin wandering about the house. I am lying on my brother's bed, in his old bedroom where I sleep. I am just lying there, thinking about life, about getting old, about my folks, and about my dad.

I remember it is Easter morn, / And life and love and peace are all new

And I think a lot about what I said – "he took me fishing."

There are two specific memories that I turn over in my mind. The first is more of a visceral memory. I am probably seven or eight. We have gotten up very early, before dawn. We would do that once in a while to get an early start when the fishing should be "better."

We are parked in front of the bait shop. It is in a grimy part of town on a dark, unlit street. I guess the bait shop must not yet have opened – I don't know why else we are sitting there.

I recall that bait shop. There were display counters with dirty glass with Eagle Claw hooks, lures, weights and the like. The fellow there would dig his hand into the big box of dirt and come out with a bunch of worms or crawlers and count them out one by one. Or he would go to the tank where there were zillions of shiners swimming about and pull out a few with his tiny net.

We are sitting in the front seat of the car. My dad has brought a thermos full of coffee. I don't recall whether I asked for a taste or he just offered. Back then, coffee was such an adult drink I don't know if I had ever tasted it before, but if I had I must not have liked it.

My dad hands me the thermos cup with coffee in it. He must have put a lot of sugar in it and a fair amount of milk. It tastes great, so warm and sweet and smooth, almost like, in retrospect, warm coffee ice cream. I have a strong visceral memory of my first taste of coffee at that moment and think of the line from the old Roger Miller chug-a-lug drinking song, "my first taste of sin."

The other memory that I turn over in my mind that night lying there on my brother's bed, way too firm for me, across the hall from my folks' bedroom, is more of a story.

I am probably twelve or thirteen, maybe fourteen. My dad and I have always tried to fish on opening day, and usually get up really early to do that. This year, I have convinced him that we ought to camp out by the trout stream where we plan to fish. I guess I have progressed a bit from bluegills and perch.

The plan, my plan which he buys into, is that we will go there the afternoon before and set up our sleeping bags, cook a simple dinner over a campfire, sleep out under the stars, get up early before the first fisherman arrives and hopefully catch a million trout.

Off we go to the stream, in a rural area maybe fifteen miles out of town. There is no campground there, just some clear space along the stream. It is late afternoon, and we set out sleeping bags, gather firewood, and get comfortable. We start our campfire and get ready to cook our dinner.

Just then, the local warden or fire chief arrives. There is too great a fire danger, we have no permit, we have to put out our fire. So, we dine that night on something like cold beans from the can, or maybe a can of sardines.

We go to sleep, get up before dawn, see some people already there and fishing. I don't remember whether we caught anything, but I think not.

Those are the two specific thoughts I have, recalling in my mind's eye (or, in the coffee story, my mind's taste buds) the episodes in more detail than the telling here.

My dad stays quiet, and I finally go to sleep.

It is the next morning. My dad is up early and wandering about the house. He thinks he is going to see the podiatrist today. I explain several times to him that, no, there is no appointment today for that. He spends a lot of time sitting on a couch in the family room. He dozes off frequently. He no longer reads the newspaper. He asks the same questions repeatedly, searches for words, and speaks a lot of confused things that have no meaning to me and make no sense. It is really all sad and upsetting.

It is late morning and I will leave in a while to go home and go to work in the office. I have to admit that I look forward to leaving, as caring for my dad is unending and tiring and not fun. He will be alone for a couple of hours until my brother gets there, but he is okay for that length of time, during the day in his own home, at least so far.

In the time I have come to spend with him, we have really had no meaningful conversations, and none of any length, except one in which he tells me he is not well, doesn't know what will happen, and asks me to take care of my mom and brother, and then another in which he tells me he has tried the best that he can. Neither of these lasts more than a couple of minutes.

I am sitting in the family room. I watch my dad doze off on that couch again. He does so with his head back, mouth open, in the typical elderly, frail fashion. He looks very, very old with just a bit of a grasp on life. I tell myself that, as I watch him there, if he suddenly stops breathing, I don't know if I'll attempt to resuscitate him.

Then he stirs, looks at me and says, "Hey, Harvey, do you remember that time we went fishing and slept out and they made us put out our campfire?"

So, what do you make of that?

I put down that I had 3 eggs... but they were Cadbury chocolate eggs."

The Tenth Plague

Barbara B. Rollins

Decades of slavery in Egypt,
a proud family become an humbled people —
how frightening the plagues, each worse,
each more oppressive.

A people terrified yet hopeful,
however slightly, to have this prince of Egypt
cum Israelite return, stand up to Pharaoh,
dare to demand freedom.

Water transforming to blood,
frogs inundating the land,
dust to lice, flies swarming,
horses, asses, camels, oxen, sheep sickening,
dust causing boils, hail pummeling the land,
locusts covering the earth, darkness three days...
What could be worse?
Death in each household!

How wondrous divine delivery
on that frightful, wondrous night.

Thanksgiving in Nebraska

R. Vern Cowles

On Thanksgiving Day, we acknowledge our dependence. ~ William Jennings Bryan

Some holidays are punctuated by sentiment, if not silly recollection. Thanksgiving inevitably comes to mind when I ponder memorable events. One of my earliest memories is visits to the "Hatterman Place," my mother's old family homestead. The Hatterman family at that time consisted of only my Uncle John and his three sisters – Mae, Minnie (my mother), and Alice – all born and raised above the North Platte River, near Broadwater in Morrill County, Nebraska. Their father had died young and the homestead was being run by Uncle John and Aunt Mildred.

After high school, Min and Alice went for one year's training at the state Normal School to become teachers in a country school. Three men from Chadron, Nebraska, began courting all three Hatterman girls, while taking courses at the college themselves. In time, they won the girls' hearts: Robert Holdeen married Mae, Arnold Cowles married Minnie, and Chuck Savidge married Alice. Aunt Alice died shortly after childbirth, and Uncle Robert later drowned saving a child from the river. This left a sad vacancy at family gatherings for some time, until Uncle Chuck and Aunt Mae eventually married and kept the family together.

My immediate family, the Cowles clan, tended to relocate every few years, as my dad, Arnold, tried on different jobs for a fit. Before our move to Alliance, Nebraska, there had been only occasional family gatherings, most of them extended family outings to public campgrounds – a place where kids could really create havoc. A cave thought to have been a hideout for Jesse James provided much diversion. One cousin brought a pickup load of watermelons, so we got our fill and accidentally split a few around the girls, splattering juice on their fancy dresses. The move to Alliance finally allowed for faithful gatherings at the Savidge home while I was in high school and beyond.

The Thanksgiving venue at Chuck and Mae's ranch house was a few miles from North Port, Nebraska, and was the closest central meeting point for us all. Several memorable celebrations come to mind here, none more clearly than the year we all convened ravenously 'round the feast table, offered a speedy prayer, and someone said, "Pass the rolls."

"Amen!" Uncle Chuck exclaimed, "Mae's holiday rolls are what Thanksgiving is all about."

Mae pushed back her seat with an "Oops" and hurried to retrieve them – only to find the oven empty. Red-faced, my mother sidled over to the refrigerator, and voilà – lovely butter-basted, chilled puffs still waiting for a ride to the oven.

Just like clockwork, my Aunt Mildred's family was always last to arrive each year. But on the positive side, their visits frequently provided a pretty female guest (in addition to cousin Verla) who was thinking about marrying one of her sons. LeRoy brought his girlfriend first (Janet, I believe), then next year Glenn, and finally Richard. This gave Chuck and Arnold – both practical jokers – a chance to meet and jibe and roundly embarrass the girls. They would always tell the young lady afterward that if she could survive their grilling, she belonged in our family. At least one of them didn't accept the offer.

Arnold and Chuck always enjoyed having a cocktail while waiting for the dinner call. Uncle Chuck invented an off-color joke every day of his adult life. It was his trademark. He'd repeat it to everyone he came in contact with. His jokes occasioned a few gasps and giggles, especially from women. The next day, he would have a different one to tell all comers.

While they caught up on things, we kids got to go exploring. We just had to see the garage where Uncle Chuck kept his secret car restorations. He had gotten started with old Model Ts picked up from farms or ranches where they were rusting away in fields. He also collected brass accessories for old autos. The basement was full of running lights, horns, bumpers and whatnots – interesting stuff for kids to see and squeeze. And meddle, we did.

Like most family gatherings, each party was expected to bring certain dishes to share – salads, casseroles and desserts. Mae cooked the turkey and dressing every year. Thanksgiving 1959 was especially memorable for her. She crawled out of bed at 4:30 a.m., trudged to the kitchen, basted and seasoned the bird and sent it off to Camp Hotpoint – forgetting to turn on the oven. "Dinner will be a bit late," she later yelled toward the living room. Mom (Minnie) frequently brought the pies for dessert. One year, Dad asked where the mincemeat pie was (his favorite), only to discover it was back home in the fridge. Of course, that meant that he could eat the whole pie later, because the rest of us Cowles family didn't like it.

These yearly gatherings continued until I was a junior in college. Sure enough, my dad moved us once again because of his work – this time as an appraiser for the federal government in Iowa. This ended our Thanksgiving gatherings. These were days of good times, full of love and laughter with family bonding. There have been many good Thanksgivings since then, but none quite so special as the ones in Nebraska.

Lost at Christmas

Judy Callarman

During the Christmas season in 1947, I was almost five years old, and my little brother Jim was barely three. We were in Fort Worth for a few days, where my grandparents lived. Our mother needed to buy one more thing for Christmas, so she took Jim and me with her to a row of stores, all decorated and glittering.

We really did not want to get out of the car, and we begged her to leave us while she went into the store just in front of the car. She agreed finally, but made us promise not to get out of the car.

Of course, after a few minutes, we were tired of the car, so we decided to go into the store and find our mother. Standing just inside the door, we couldn't see that she was near the back of the store. We thought she must be in the store next door. We went into the next store, and the next, and the next, looking for her.

Puzzled and upset, we crossed a street. I held Jim's hand, as a good big sister should. We walked and walked and soon found ourselves in a neighborhood. We realized then that we had to go back to the car. We went around a block or two.

We were completely lost. Jim started to wail, and I was on the verge of tears myself, but I was the older one; I thought I had to be calm and responsible and think through our situation. But then I started to cry, too.

Suddenly the navy-blue-clad legs of a large policeman were in front of us. Startled, we looked up at his kind face. "Are you Jim and Judy?" he asked. We gulped and nodded. We were found. Our mother was close behind him, and she was crying harder than we were. I didn't understand why she was crying, since she was not the one who was lost.

I thought we had to find our way back. I had no idea anyone would be looking for us, and I thought I was responsible for Jim. Mother had been searching for us since the moment she discovered we were gone. She loved us that much.

This year, I realize how my Christmas experience as a desperate lost child is a parable of the experiences of every sad, lonely, hopeless person. Jesus, born in a stable somewhere around two thousand years ago, is the shepherd, the father – the large, kind policeman in blue – who searches for every lost child and calls each one by name. We do not have to find our own way to love, peace, safety and joy, because he is looking for us.

Thanksgiving

It has been said that Thanksgiving is the only truly American holiday. Traditionally, it is the day set aside to commemorate the hardships the Pilgrims faced trying to settle in America. The Pilgrims themselves set aside a time for celebration of their harvests, to express gratitude to God for their bounty, and to share their fruits with Native Americans who had befriended them and taught them. Indeed, it is a day to celebrate community and cooperation, to show appreciation for one another, a day for counting blessings.

The first Thanksgiving celebration included feasting for three full days. According to history, more than ninety Native Americans joined the Pilgrims in their celebration. Their feast included native game and foods, including venison, turkeys, corn and squash. The gathering served as a gesture of goodwill for both parties.

Thanksgiving was not immediately adopted as an American holiday. In the mid-nineteenth century, Sarah Joseph Hale thought the celebration to be a valuable tradition and petitioned President Abraham Lincoln and other officials to make Thanksgiving a national holiday. Her words were heard, moving President Lincoln in 1863 to proclaim the last Thursday of November as a day to celebrate Thanksgiving.

In 1939, President Franklin D. Roosevelt affirmed the proclamation that Thanksgiving should be held as a national holiday and decreed the fourth Thursday of November as the official date for national observance. In 1941 congress declared Thanksgiving as an official federal holiday, retaining the assignment of date to the fourth Thursday of November.

Traditions and icons

- Macy's Thanksgiving Day Parade
- hometown parades and celebrations
- family gatherings and special meals – traditionally turkey
- giving thanks for personal blessings
- watching football games

A Family Seder

B.J. Yudelson

My husband Julian and I beam from opposite ends of the table. Children and grandchildren range on either side, cousins vying to sit near cousins they rarely see. We have each selected a Haggadah, the book that contains the order of the Passover Seder, from a wide selection collected over the years. Some have interesting commentary, others feature beautiful illustrations. The younger children hold the ones they made in school. Julian's red and yellow paperback edition is wine-stained, dog-eared, and dotted with handwritten notes that reflect his thoughts as leader through the years. In it he has also recorded the names of our guests, or hosts, for every Seder since 1974.

"What do we do first?" he asks. "Who knows the order of the Seder?"

"I do! I do!" calls out Calanit, five, our youngest granddaughter.

"Can you sing it?" prompts Grandpa.

Her cousin Ruthie, seven, a born performer, starts in a high voice. *"Kadesh, urhatz..."* We all join her to chant the order of the Passover Seder.

We pour wine or grape juice for each other – free people never pour their own! – and recite kiddush, the blessing over wine. I picture Joey two years ago when Larry asked his then-six-year-old son to read the Hebrew. Joey complied, we said "amen" and drank our wine. Joey looked up in surprise, "Did I just say kiddush?" Now he, and all his siblings and cousins, read Hebrew more fluently than their grandparents.

This has to be one of the longest Seders ever! "What is there to discuss?" my father once asked. Let's see: Why do we wash our hands without saying a blessing? Why do we eat a green vegetable? Why did my family use parsley and Julian's, potatoes? Why is the phrase, "All who are hungry – let them come and eat," written in Aramaic, not Hebrew? To every question, someone has an answer, and often another question as well. The children pipe up with interpretations they learned in their Jewish day schools in New Jersey and California. The teenagers give more thoughtful interpretations, ask more sophisticated questions. "What is the relationship between law and freedom?" "Suppose the Exodus never happened... would we be Jewish today?" "Why do the men get all the credit?"

I think of my father's question – Which is more important, honoring your parents or keeping the Sabbath? – and am grateful that these grand-children seem to take seriously both the ethical and ritual sides of Judaism. Only time will tell how they will balance them and how they will respond intellectually and spiritually to their birthright.

We recite the ten plagues, using our baby fingers or a fork to spill a drop of wine or grape juice for each plague. Sam, fifteen, explains, "This sym-bolizes our sadness at the loss of human life, even our enemies. We can't be totally happy about the plagues when we know that so many Egyptians died when they followed the Israelites into the sea."

"That's right," our son Larry responds. "We don't rejoice in others' misfortune, even when it helps us."

And, a few pages later, "How thankful must we be to God, the All-Present, for all the good He did for us." We sing in rousing Hebrew,

"Had He brought us out from Egypt
And not executed judgment against them,
Di-ayenu, It would have been enough for us!"
Multiple verses later, we conclude,
"Had He brought us to the Land of Israel
And not built for us the Holy Temple,
Di-aynu, It would have been enough for us!
Di-di-aynu, Di-aynu, Di-ay-nu!"

Finally, we are ready for the festive meal. My daughter Miriam, daughter-in-law Eve, and the older girls help me serve okra soup for the vegetarians as well as traditional chicken soup, brisket and turkey, matzah farfel stuffing, carrots, asparagus, and salad.

"Whoever says there are no good desserts during Passover hasn't tasted Grandma's baking," says Yael, our eldest granddaughter.

"All your wonderful assistance makes them even better." Preparing a Seder with my grandchildren's help is this Grandma's dream.

With children on two coasts, we are seldom all together. This year, when both Julian and I turn seventy, we have brought all the children and grandchildren to Rochester for a joint celebration.

For me, the high point of this week comes at lunch the second day when Miriam says to the children, "You know, we're not just three generations in this room."

"We're not?" asks Kinneret, ten.

"Behind me is my great-great...how many greats, Mom?"

"That woman in the astounding Bavarian headdress is my great-great-great-grandmother, so four greats for you," I reply.

Miriam points to another portrait. "And over there is Granny, my great-grandmother."

"You were so lucky to know your great-grandmother!" Aviva, nine, chimes in.

"Yes," agrees Miriam. "She lived 'til 103. I was eleven when she died, so I have very clear memories of her." Miriam gestures toward a painting of an old French peasant woman holding a Seder plate with the same symbols we have cherished this week. "And that lady isn't a relative. But from the time I was your age, I've seen her as offering me the tradition. I wouldn't dare not accept it!"

I had no idea that Miriam felt that way about my Seder Lady, a gift from my aunt when my daughter was only seven. I love this work by Alfonse Levy, who, like my great-grandfather, was from Alsace-Lorraine. On the French-German border, the territory went back and forth between the two countries. It was French during the period between my great-grandfather Moses Blum's 1830 birth and his 1849 emigration to America.

"Did you know," I ask Miriam, "that the artist did a whole series of these Alsatian peasants to preserve at least a memory of the Jewish customs that he assumed were disappearing?"

"Disappearing? I guess we're proving him wrong – aren't we, kids?"

As my grandchildren nod their acceptance of the tradition I have climbed rung by rung to reclaim from my nontraditional upbringing, I look up at the portrait of Granny, Moses Blum's daughter. Thank you, I think, for being my bookmark. If you hadn't maintained at least social ties to Judaism, where would I be today? Probably not at a Passover table surrounded by grandchildren who assume traditional Judaism as their legacy.

Christmas Baby's First Board Book

Ginny Greene

In the short poem below, I left out presents wrapped half-Christmas/half-birthday, the birthday cake we were always too full for, and the names people thought I should be named (Carol, Holly, Noelle).

Later in life, my kids and grandkids gave me half-birthdays in July so it could be my own special day.

I also wanted to acknowledge the many others I know who have birthdays eclipsed by special days. So, distilled, I offer a statement on learning to share birthdays with The Big Guy.

This,
Little One,
is Christmas.
After church, presents, singing 'round the piano, family dinner, and just before cake —
This,
now,
is your birthday.

Christmas

Christmas in all countries around the world celebrates the birth of Jesus. According to the Bible, Jesus was born unto Mary and Joseph, poor Jews who were fleeing possible persecution. In Bethlehem, where they found shelter, the child was visited by three kings – all bearing gifts. The event heralded the dawn of a new day in human history and a religious movement known as Christianity – after Jesus the Christ (messiah). Celebrations of Jesus' birth may vary among world cultures, but the core event and the biblical account is permanent and universal.

In recent centuries, a parallel secular Christmas celebration has evolved in which a Santa Claus figure has emerged as the central theme. There are various accounts of Santa's origin. During the sixth century, a Catholic bishop named Saint Nicholas is said to have been generous to the poor and very kindly to children. By 540 A.D. he was known as the "saint of children and gift giving." The Dutch celebrated a man named "Sinterklass," who rode a white horse and carried a big sack of gifts over his shoulder. In Great Britain, a kindly figure known as Father Christmas – who was jolly and went about in a green suit – became a prominent part of Christmas.

One early description of modern Santa Claus appeared in an 1821 poem by William Gilley – Santa dressed in fur and being pulled in a sleigh by reindeer. A year later, Clement Clark Moore wrote his famous story, "A Visit from St. Nicholas" – which became more widely known as "Twas the Night Before Christmas." In 1863, well-known artist Thomas Nast began painting annual pictures of Santa. Eventually, even Coca Cola capitalized on the Santa craze in their ads.

Traditions and icons include

- nativity scenes, crèches
- *The Nutcracker*
- fruitcake, candy canes, holiday foods
- plays and reenactments of the holy birth
- cantatas and caroling in the streets
- hometown Christmas parades
- decorated trees, wreaths, holiday lights, mistletoe, holly
- gift giving, Christmas cards
- Christmas stockings
- Santa Claus

Grappling with Ghosts

Pat Butler

I am jarred awake by a leaf-blower. I look out the bedroom window and see a neighbor migrating up and down his sidewalk, clearing paths everywhere. A gray sky is lowering to fill the bare arms of the late autumn trees. Kids are scurrying home from school like so many leaves in the wind – it's Halloween!

Another neighbor is setting up cornstalks along his fence, and another, across the street, is loading his yard with ghosts, goblins, skeletons, tombstones and pumpkins. Witches and bats fly from his trees. Soon a full moon will rise – for the first time on Halloween in forty-six years. Anticipation rises with the stiffening breeze, growing colder and stronger as twilight descends.

I'm visiting my sister and her family, and it's just another Halloween. But it's been a while since I've lived through one, having spent the last several years overseas. How is it celebrated now? The neighbors seem obsessed with their decorations, the kids are at a fever pitch, and I am curious. Just another Halloween, with a difference: I'm excited.

work." Thomas Edison ~§~ "Remember this day, on which you went

My excitement confuses me. Halloween is not what it used to be. As fear, commercialism, and religious polemic replaced fun, magic and innocence, I grew to hate the holiday. I have boycotted the holiday for years – partly because I am more aware of spiritual realities, partly because I resist the commercial manipulation, partly because I just don't like skeletons, witches and demonic masks. So this growing excitement betrays me.

I'm living the holiday through the eyes of my sister's children – reliving the ghosts of Halloweens past. Costumes, decorations, friends, spookiness, the crisp night air, skirting the big boys roaming the neighborhood with eggs and shaving cream, amassing all that free candy – what's not to like?

Perhaps it is because I am sick and therefore have a "day off" – confined to bed, a complete luxury after a month of work-related travel. Though the body is weak, the spirit is as freed as the children's. I get to rest, read, write, sip tea and watch Halloween from my ringside seat at my street-level window – so much time, with all those travels and experiences to digest, a notebook full of ideas to write about, and a holiday to do it in. Somewhere inside me I decide not to resolve the existential question of Halloween tonight, but simply enjoy it. Perhaps this is compromise, but so be it. I'm sick, and too tired to argue with myself.

Darkness descends and with it, my nephew Matt, who jumps on my bed with his goody bag from school and a torrent of words. Into my lap he

free from Egypt, the house of bondage, how Adonai freed you from

pours candy, an egg-carton witch's head, and a bat stencil. He roots for other treasure to give me until Grandma arrives to shoo him away from my germs.

Next comes niece Stephanie. We discuss briefly the pros and cons of the holiday, but I can tell by the glaze in her eyes that I should drop the subject. Though I am duty-bound to guide my goddaughter in matters of faith and morals, perhaps this isn't the moment. The lure of candy overpowers all consideration of good and evil. Instead, our discussion rapidly turns to the pros and cons of the ideal candy-gathering sack: pillowcase or brown paper bag with handles? Pillowcase wins. Grandma, ever vigilant, returns to chase Stephanie out.

At 5:30 the doorbell rings and I hear a rush for the door – first customer! No – false alarm. Stephanie's friend has come to borrow makeup for her costume. Much to Grandma's horror, I emerge from my room – germs and all – to check out the costumes, take some pictures, and eat pumpkin seeds. The germs may have kept me from the pumpkin carving last night, but I won't miss the pumpkin seeds tonight. Brian, Master Pumpkin Seed Roaster, makes the best. Taking the scooped-out seeds from the pumpkins, he sprays them with olive oil and bakes them, just right, before serving them on a royal blue platter. We feast, then collect the pumpkins from the back porch, and position them on the front stoop, in size order.

At 6:15 a swarm of friends arrives: Harry Potter, a witch, a fairy, a SWAT team. "It's an eerie night," declares Matt, pointing at the swarm with his left ear, over which he has looped a hollowed-out piece of Italian bread.

The swarm collects Matt and Steph, and swarms back out, across the street, where ghosts and goblins swirl in the trees. Bats blink in the branches, lights garnish the bushes, and the neighbor emerges, now a hooded, black-robed ghoul, wielding a scythe. The kids squeal in delight. A car stops, and a crowd forms. I expect a news crew to arrive any second.

The doorbell sounds regularly and frequently now. My sister clops back and forth in her heels, a tray of goody bags in hand, trying to identify the trick-or-treaters before her. One group of giddy girls giggles, "Have we been here before? We forget which houses we've gone to…"

Eight thirty: the frenzy calms, surprisingly early. Stephanie and Matt return and spill the contents of their pillowcases on the floor. "This is the best part!" says Steph, as she and Matt begin sorting and bartering like seasoned merchants. We adults hover like vultures, eyeing our favorite candies as they are traded, wondering how to get at the booty. Eventually, the kids finish their barter, and toss us the rejects, offering one chocolate bar of choice before closing negotiations and disappearing to their bedrooms. Halloween, for better or worse, is over.

But my question lingers. For someone who had grown to hate Halloween, why was I enjoying it so much?

Sometimes it is only in eating a meal that you realize how hungry you are. Only after Halloween ended did I realize how starved I was for a different type of meal: of magic, drama, theater, mystery, wonder, imagination. My nephew and niece, with their friends, brought me back to the feast. They brought me back to a time before one bought overpriced store costumes or knew about vampires, demons and witches. They took me to a time before Halloween was denounced in some quarters and "harvest parties" were substituted – an anemic response to the imagination of every child planning a Halloween costume and plotting a route for maximal candy collecting.

I reverted to a time when I could dress up like a clown, stay up past my bedtime, and eat too much candy – before I became a dutiful adult.

When did it become too time-consuming to play?

Halloween has its charms: autumn colors, mums, yellow leaves, apples, cider, pumpkins, family times, friends, creating costumes, dressing up, going out in the dark, hiding, running, chasing, disrupting routine.

Its evil overtones remind us at least that there is evil, an invisible world, an unseen reality, spirits we perceive with the eyes of our hearts. Those eyes need to be opened regularly, especially as we get older; magic and wonder can do the trick! And when our eyes are fully open, we also see Good.

I think I still oppose Halloween on principle. But I see the Good. This Halloween, my eyes cleared enough to see and re-enter the land of imagination. It was a great visit.

The made-from-scratch holiday

Ginny Greene

In a car full of kids and Off! and picnic lunch and just-in-case coats, we set off on a glorious autumn Saturday for a day at Mount Rainier.

All the long drive, we pictured an ice-cream cone mountain glittering scenically. Mt. Rainier is high and broad and forever snowy, and even the slightest view in the distance lifts a Seattle soul above its cloud cover. The mountain has many moods – from glittering to shadow – and often creates its own weather. On different days or different hours it wears anything from a flat white cap to a heavy poncho shroud. We could never be sure the same mountain, visible when we packed the car, would be clear or cloaked by the time we got there.

But we were ready for the adventure, fueled by the memory of previous hikes and picnics and a chance to set our webbed and water-logged feet on a mountain path.

Not long on the road, the kids began to wonder aloud, *How long? Are we there yet?* That, of course, is part of an outing with kids, so we kept going. But deep into the foothills, we stopped for a minute, just to stretch our legs and let the kids get their wiggles out. It was just a pull-out space off the road.

The sun peeked through the trees, warming our bodies and our hopes. It sat on the arms of evergreens and dappled the ground beneath leafy trees. The roadside was golden, infused with a serenity of autumn hue.

We stepped onto a thick quilt, a crisp cushioning of gold and ochre and red. I kicked some of the leaves, enjoying the dry crunching sound. A breeze picked up on the game and sent a trail of color skittering a few inches aloft. A bird chirped its approval. The wind tickled the tops of trees, raining down more crinkly leaves. We walked deeper into the woods, lured by the magic of autumn's oblique light.

Someone mentioned a "remember when?" This place was the perfect setting for the backward glance of memory. We wandered and kicked more leaves. Someone else added to the story. It was our family story, recalled and told from the per-spective of each child and parent and cousin and aunt. The memories were woven and laced together in a tight-knit story, shaping a story of depth and brilliance to hang on the walls of our minds.

In a still moment, someone's stomach growled. We did a quick calculation of how long it would be to the mountain. We were torn by the choice to accept this spontaneous *Now*, or persist in our goal. But all chose to lunch in this spot that had welcomed us unexpectedly beside the road.

Our holiday is not a national day of remembrance. It shaped and spun itself out of leaves and light and eager hearts and separate memories woven together. The mountain was still alluring, somewhere over several hilltops, but we came away from that roadside stop with a beautiful sense of destination, and the desire to make autumn leaf-kicking, somewhere along a mountain road, an annual family holiday.

About the Authors

Marie Asner is an entertainment reviewer, poet, freelance writer and workshop presenter with over 5500 bylines. She has been a regular radio guest in the Midwest as a film critic. Marie is also a church musician, recipient of a writing grant for an Amelia Earhart poetry project and current Kansas Senior Poet Laureate.

Carol Ayer's poetry has been published by *Poetry Quarterly, Poesia, Every Day Poets*, and in previous *Silver Boomer Books*. Her other credits include *Woman's World, The Christian Science Monitor*, and several *Chicken Soup for the Soul* volumes. Carol lives in Northern California and works as a freelance writer. Visit her website at *www.carolayer.com*.

Debra Ayers Brown is a writer, humorist, blogger, magazine columnist, and award-winning marketing professional. Enjoy her stories in *Guideposts; Woman's World; Liberty Life Magazine; Chicken Soup for the Soul; Chocolate for Women; Not Your Mother's Book*, and more. She is a University of Georgia honor graduate with her MBA from The Citadel. Debra, "proud momma" of daughter Meredith, lives near Savannah, Georgia, with her husband Allen and mother Sara. Visit her at *DebraAyersBrown.com*.

Cathy Bryant's poems and stories have been published all over the world in magazines and anthologies. In 2010 she won the Marple Humorous Poetry Prize; in 2012 she won the Sampad "Inspired by Tagore" Poetry Contest and the Swanezine Poetry Competition and became runner-up Prole Laureate. Cathy co-edits the annual anthology *Best of Manchester Poets*. Her own collection, *Contains Strong Language and Scenes of a Sexual Nature,would* is available from all good booksellers or online. She can be contacted at cathy@cathybryant.co.uk.

Janelle Burch lives in Southeast Missouri and is a member and past president of the Heartland Writers Guild. She has placed in contests for a children's story and photography. She is a teacher and educational supervisor in the field of severe disabilities and enjoys writing short stories relevant to life in small towns, articles on the subject of genealogy and children's stories.

Pat Butler grew up on Long Island, New York, where holidays revolved around beaches, boats and clam shacks. Leaving the island as a young adult, Pat opted for city living in New England and France, traveling widely while rediscovering her roots through other cultures. Currently residing near Atlanta, Georgia, Pat is exploring Southern culture and literature, while continuing to write, travel and enjoy any activity near the ocean. Previous publication credits include *Fresh Boiled Peanuts, Rhythm & Rhyme 6, Ruminate*, and online magazines. Her first poetry chapbook, *Poems from the Boatyard,* was published by Finishing Line Press (*www.finishinglinepress.com*) in 2011. Blog: *poems fromtheboatyard.blogspot.com.*

Judy Callarman lives in Cisco, Texas. She is a retired professor of creative writing and English at Cisco College and chair of the Fine Arts Division. Her poems and nonfiction have won contests and been published in Silver Boomer Books' *This Path* and *From the Porch Swing; Radix; Passager; Grandmother Earth;* and *Patchwork Path – Christmas Stocking.*

Loretta Carter lives in a community called Hanging Dog in Murphy, North Carolina. She is married with three grown daughters and five grandchildren. She is retired from a local hospital where she worked in the business office for close to twenty-five years. She is a new writer but has been interested in writing since her high school days.

Mary Chandler is a prolific writer whose work has appeared in many magazines, journals, zines, newspapers, anthologies, and on the Internet. A retired teacher and avid reader, she also enjoys travel, meeting new people, and visiting with family and friends. Mary lives in Reno, Nevada. She and her husband are parents to three wonderful children and five fabulous grandkids!

Madonna Dries Christensen lives in Sarasota, Florida, with her husband, Gary Christensen. Three times nominated for the Pushcart Prize and recipient of other writing awards, Madonna is Editor/Publisher of *Doorways* magazine; a columnist for *Extra Innings*, and Contributing Editor to *Yesterday's Magazette* and *Writer's Magazette*. Her published books are *Swinging Sisters; Masquerade: The Swindler Who Conned J. Edgar Hoover; The Quiet Warrior; Dolls Remembered;* and *Toys Remembered*. A collection of her memoirs, *In Her Shoes: Step by Step*, was published in 2012. All books are available through Amazon and other major bookstores. Royalties go to chosen organizations. Website: *www.madonnadrieschristensen.com.*

Beth Lynn Clegg, Houston, Texas, is an octogenarian who began her writing career after retiring from other endeavors. She has been published in a variety of genres, and also enjoys cooking, gardening, reading, and church activities. Her favorite activity is spending time with family, friends, and two spoiled cats.

R. Vern Cowles was a native Nebraskan who recently retired as Los Angeles County Registrar of Voters. He held dual Masters degrees in Economics (Doane College) and Theology (Washington University) and was published in religious and education magazines, including *The Episcopal News* and *Reading Improvement,* and in the holiday anthology, *Thanksgiving to Christmas: A Patchwork of Stories.*

Kerry Alan Denney has been writing short stories, novels and songs, and playing guitar and trumpet since before he was old enough to shave. He has independently released three "project" CDs full of evocative melodies and provocative six-string shred-dage, and is the First Place Winner of the Atlanta Writers Club Fall 2009 Poetry Contest. Although he believes but cannot prove that the Easter Bunny and the Tooth Fairy are sinister fabrications of a vast capitalist conspiracy, he still fervently believes in Santa Claus. His author's website is *www.kerrydenney.com.*

Terri Elders, LCSW, lives near Colville, Washington. She's a frequent contributor to anthologies, with over fifty pieces of creative nonfiction appearing in books such as *Chicken Soup for the Soul, Thin Threads* and *God Makes Lemonade*. She currently is a co-creator and editor for Publishing Syndicate's new anthology series, *Not Your Mother's Book.* A public member of the Washington State Medical Quality Assurance Commission, Terri received UCLA's 2006 Alumni Award for Community Service for her work with Peace Corps. She's lived in Belize, Guatemala, Dominican Republic and Seychelles. She blogs at *atouchof tarragon.blogspot.com.*

Joanne Faries, originally from the Philadelphia area, lives in Texas with her husband Ray. Published in *Doorknobs & Bodypaint,* she also has poems in *Magnapoets* and Silver Boomer Books anthologies. Joanne is the film critic for *The Little Paper of San Saba.* Look for her humorous memoir *My Zoo World: If All Dogs Go to Heaven, Then I'm in Trouble* on Amazon. *Wordsplash-joannefaries.blogspot.com.*

Marilyn E. Freeman lives in Florida. She has two daughters, ten wonderful grandchildren and one adorable great-grandson. She is the author of two children's books, *Summer Adventures With Grandma* and *Pasquale's Journey.* She has been published in several magazines. Her anthology work has been published by Blooming Tree Press, Patchwork Path, Write Integrity Press, and a story in *Hurray God, Hope Pray Believe.*

Cynthia Gallaher is the author of three published collections of poetry and is on Chicago Public Library's list of "Top Ten Requested Chicago Poets." She teaches online journal writing classes through the University of Illinois at Chicago Writers Series, and leads creative writing workshops at libraries, centers and park districts. Gallaher's holiday poems are part of a larger manuscript called *Holiday Palooza.* Follow her on Twitter at *twitter.com/ swimmerpoet.*

Jeannette Clift George is the founder/artistic director of the A.D. Players, the Houston-based Christian Theater Company. Jeannette is equally well known as author, playwright, Bible teacher, national speaker and star of the movie *The Hiding Place.*

Ginny Greene wrote newspaper features, became a columnist, and edited several newsletters before settling beside a river in Idaho. She is a past president of Abilene Writers Guild,

country they accepted death." James A. Garfield ~§~ "The legacy of and one of the original four partners of Silver Boomer Books. She is an avid fan of words and continues as a freelance writer and editor.

Ginny's book *Song of County Roads* was published by Silver Boomer Books in 2009. She is working to complete two more volumes of nonfiction, pleading daily with her computer to cooperate.

Becky Haigler is a founding partner in Silver Boomer Books and author of the short story collection *Not so GRIMM: gentle fables and cautionary tales*. Retired from teaching Spanish in Texas public schools, Becky follows her husband Dave wherever his work takes him. She is a mother and grandmother and dabbler in arts and crafts of various kinds, though she prefers the term "Renaissance woman."

Dixon Hearne's work has been twice nominated for the Pushcart Prize and the Hemingway Foundation/PEN Award. His recent book, *Plantatia: High-toned and Lowdown Stories of the South*, received the Creative Spirit-Platinum award for Best Fiction Book. Other work appears in *Mature Living, Louisiana Literature, Cream City Review, Wisconsin Review*, and numerous other magazines, journals, and anthologies. His work also appears in two previous Silver Boomer Books anthologies: *Flashlight Memories* and *From the Porch Swing*.

Elizabeth Howard lives in Crossville, Tennessee. She writes both poetry and fiction. Her stories have been published in *Xavier Review, Elixir, Appalachian Heritage, The Distillery, Wind, Muscadine Lines, Still,* and other journals.

Janet Klise is a retired writer-editor-photographer, having fulfilled these duties for more than 40 years for high school, college, university, and federal government publications. After so many years of loving to read, write and edit, she finds she cannot leave the reading and writing alone. She limits editing to her own writing and to Letters to the Editor. Janet was born in Monroe, Louisiana, but has lived in California since the age of four. She now resides with her husband Tim and cats, Callie, Cairo and Alice, in Clovis, California.

Nancy Julien Kopp grew up in Chicago but has lived in the Flint Hills of Kansas for many years. She and her retired husband enjoy traveling and attending Kansas State University sports events and family gatherings. Although she started writing late in life, Nancy has been published in twelve *Chicken Soup for the Soul* books, several other anthologies, including *Flashlight Memories* at Silver Boomer Books, ezines, newspapers and magazines. She is an occasional poet. Once a classroom teacher, she now teaches through the written word. Visit her blog at *www.writergrannysworld.blogspot.com.*

MaryEllen Letarte, wife, mother, and grandmother, writes stories and poems while sitting at a cluttered desk in Lunenburg, Massachusetts, USA. She is founder and director of the Louise Bogan Chapter of the Massachusetts State Poetry Society. Her poems and stories have appeared online and in national publications, including Silver Boomer Books. Visit *versealive. wordpress.com* and *www.louisebogan.com.*

Carrie McClure is an actor and woman of many talents who savors life one day at a time with her cat, Rosie. Now a resident of St. Louis, she won critics' awards for her acting while living in Dallas. Her poetry has appeared in the Silver Boomer Books anthology *From the Porch Swing.*

Kyle McLoflin is a southern poet by nature and dairy farmer by circumstance. His roots run six generations deep in the Louisiana delta. Legend has that his forebears blew into New Orleans on the tail winds of a hurricane in 1817. He spends his leisure time crafting poems and rifling through genealogical records for evidence of connections to royalty. Thus far, his closest connections are two regal pups, Duke and Countess.

Carole Ann Molett's memoir, *Someday I'm Going To Write a Book: Diary of an Urban Missionary*, chronicles her experiences as a public health nurse in the inner city. Excerpts have appeared in *This Path, Thanksgiving to Christmas: A Patchwork of Stories* and *Oasis Journal,* which awarded Carole its prize for Best Nonfiction in 2009.

example." Benjamin Disraeli ~§~ "Easter spells out beauty, the rare

Wilda Morris is Workshop Chair of Poets & Patrons of Chicago and former President of the Illinois State Poetry Society. She has won numerous awards, including a Pushcart nomination. Her work has been published in numerous anthologies and journals (both print and online). Her book, *Szechwan Shrimp and Fortune Cookies: Poems from a Chinese Restaurant,* was published by RWG Press. Each month, Wilda Morris's Poetry Challenge provides a contest for other poets on her blog at *wildamorris.blogspot.com.* She also offers leadership for poetry workshops in various locations.

Sheryl L. Nelms is from Marysville, Kansas. She graduated from South Dakota State University in Family Relations and Child Development. She has had over 5,000 articles, stories and poems published, including fourteen individual collections of her poems. She is the fiction/nonfiction editor of *The Pen Woman Magazine,* the National League of American Pen Women publication, and a recent Pushcart Prize nominee. Sheryl's *Bluebonnets, Boots and Buffalo Bones* was published by the Laughing Cactus Press imprint of Silver Boomer Books.

The Rev. Dr. Bill Olewiler is a retired United Methodist pastor from Virginia. He earned his M.Div, M.R.E. and Doctor of Ministry degrees from Wesley Theological Seminary, Washington, DC. He is the former Pastor of Asbury United Methodist Church, Orange Park, Florida, and is an Affiliate Member of the Florida Annual Conference. He led Community UMC, Lake Como, from December 2010 to June 2011. Bill and Nancy Payne-Olewiler have been married for four years. Nancy is from Illinois, and Bill and Nancy are members of the Rockford Writers' Guild, Rockford, Illinois.

Carl Palmer, twice nominated for the Micro Award and thrice for the Pushcart Prize by poetry magazine editors, is from Old Mill Road in Ridgeway, Virginia. Carl now lives in University Place, Washington. MOTTO: Long Weekends Forever!

Joan Peronto lives in New England but is a transplanted midwesterner, having graduated from the U. of Wisconsin, Madison. She worked as a reference librarian for 30 years and has been published in *Crossing Paths,* an anthology of western New

England poets, *The Berkshire Review, The Berkshire Sampler, Hummingbird* and *The Rockford Review.*

Barbara B. Rollins, writer, editor and publisher with Silver Boomer Books, takes advice from her sons and husband when they are right and explores what she chooses – her favorite activity being hugging twin grandsons. Her Eagle Wings Press books *A Time for Verse – Poetic Ponderings on Ecclesiastes* and *A Cloud of Witnesses – Two Big Books and Us,* added to a series of juvenile forensic books and the young adult novel *Syncopated Summer,* make this anthology the fifteenth book bearing her name.

Stan Rosenberg was a founding director of the Tupelo Press, a member of the League of Vermont Writers, Manchester Dance, and a board member of the Manchester Music Festival. Though born in Brooklyn, New York, a good portion of Stan's youth was happily spent on his grandfather's farm in upstate New York. He has been a pharmacist, stockbroker and innkeeper. Now a longtime resident of Vermont, his work has appeared in *The Manchester Journal* and *Lost Magazine.*

Sioux Roslawski is a third grade teacher, a dog rescuer for Love a Golden, and a freelance writer. Her quirky musings can be found at *siouxspage.blogspot.com.* She's been published in several *Chicken Soup for the Soul* anthologies, and is currently working with an illustrator on a picture book entitled *A Home for Always.*

Harvey Silverman is a retired physician living in Manchester, New Hampshire. He writes primarily for his own enjoyment, but his nonfiction has appeared in both professional and general publications.

Pat St. Pierre has been writing poetry, fiction, and nonfiction since her college days. She tries to capture small vignettes of life and turn them into poems. Her second chapbook, *Theater of Life,* published by Finishing Line Press, contains such poems. Her poems have been widely published in such places as *Boston Literary Review, Three Line Poetry,* Silver Boomer Books, *The Shine Journal, The Camel Saloon, Flutter Poetry,* and *Wind.* Pat

ables a normal human being to do the impossible." Marrion C. Gar-

loves photography and can be seen carrying her camera wherever she goes. She takes photos which also describe "snapshots" of everyday occurrences. Some of her photos can be viewed at *Ken*Again, Ramshackle Review, Pond Ripples, The Shine, The Camel Saloon,* and *Decades.* She considers herself a literary "jack of all trades" and thoroughly enjoys what she does. Her blog is *www.pstpierre.wordpress.com.*

Suki Stone is a reading specialist for children and mentor for doctoral students in the San Diego area. She is currently working on a book about reading and language arts instruction for students with learning disabilities. She writes poetry and is an open-mic poetry host at local bookstores and coffee houses.

Susan Sundwall writes from her home in upstate New York. She's a freelance writer and mystery novelist. Her first novel, *The Red Shoelace Killer – A Minnie Markwood Mystery* (Mainly Murder Press) will be available on November 1, 2012. Her numerous poems, essays, and articles have been published in *Ideals, Sasee, Catholic Forester* and *Funds for Writers,* among many others. Go on over to her blog at *www.susansundwall.blogspot. com* and find out what else she's been up to.

Diane Tarantini lives in a hundred-year-old house in Morgantown, West Virginia. She is a graduate of West Virginia University's Perry Isaac Reed School of Journalism. Her writing has won awards in humor, inspiration, and book-length prose. Recently she had a revelation that she is a writer, not a novelist, preferring to work in the under-5,000-word realm. Now she must determine whether or not to burn her 90,000-word not-quite-memoir manuscript in the *chiminea* out back.

B.J. Yudelson, a retired writer for not-for-profit agencies, writes creative nonfiction in Rochester, New York. Her work has appeared in *Colere, Democrat & Chronicle, Eclectica Magazine, The Griffin, Jewish Action, The Jewish Georgian, The Legendary, Tiny Lights,* and the anthology *Flashlight Memories.* Both of her pieces in *A Quilt of Holidays* are excerpted from her memoir, which she is currently revising for the umpteenth time.

Attributions

The following selections included in *A Quilt of Holidays* were previously published as noted below. The authors retain all copyright to the work.

"Dad's Special Gift," *Grit*, December 10, 2000; *When Christmas Comes to Our House*, 2002 (Weems Concepts); *A Cup of Comfort for Christmas*, September 2003, Adams Media, under the title "Priceless, Timeless" ~§~ "A Most Distinguished Effect," *Yesterdays Magazette*, December 2008; *In Her Shoes*, 2012 ~§~ "Brown Bags and Christmas Paper," *Christmas is a Season* (2008) ~§~ "Christmas Cactus," *The Shepherd*, December 2006 ~§~ "Christmas Puzzle," *Prairie Times* (2011) ~§~ "Easter Bloomers," *Chicken Soup for the Soul, Celebrating Brothers and Sisters*, October 2007 ~§~ "Flag Day Thoughts," a shorter version, *The Best of Times; OurEcho.com* ~§~ "Independence Day in Chicago," *OurEcho.com* ~§~ "In Keeping with Christmas Past," *Yesterday's Magazette*, December 2007; *In Her Shoes*, 2012 ~§~ "Konawa in Time for Christmas," *Patchwork Path: Christmas Stocking* ~§~ "Kumquats," Trinity Writer's Workshop *Christmas in the Stockyards*, 2010 ~§~ "Lost at Christmas," *Eastland County Newspapers*, December 2011 ~§~ "Once Upon an Easter," *The Shepherd*, March 2007 ~§~ "Plain and Simple Hearts," *Yesterday's Magazette; In Her Shoes,* 2012 ~§~ "The Redhead and the Tiger Lily," *Montana Senior News*, April/May 1999; *Carefree Enterprise,* March 2001; *RPPS* (Fullosia Press), March 17, 2007, Internet publication ~§~ "The Rudolph Sweater," *Christmas Traditions*, Adams Media, 2009 ~§~ "The Secret Ingredient," *The Embrace of a Father:True Stories of Inspiration and Encouragement* (Bethany House, 2006) ~§~ "Shepherd in an Old Bathrobe," *Discovery Trails*, December 12, 1999 ~§~ "Thanksgiving in Nebraska," *Thanksgiving to Christmas: A Patchwork of Stories* (2009) ~§~ "Thanksgiving is..." *Thanksgiving Tales* anthology ~§~ "Zola's Flowers," *Liguorian*, May/June 2004; *RPPS* (Fullosia Press) April/May 2007, Internet publication; *Inky Trail News*, July/August 2010 ~§~ "He Took Me Fishing" *Australian Readers Digest,* September 2012

Nice Dramatic Pauses

The Ensemble

I also vote for dash.
You get nice dramatic pauses —
with dashes.

It's a short, essential appositive.
Rules say don't separate verbs
and objects by colons.
I know, I know, it's very picky!
That makes it a run-on or comma-splice.
Praps I'll send it.

I think we have enough Easter without her.
Agreed. She did get tiresome.
Out she goes.
My alter-ego bio is pretty boring.

One thing that bothers me about this piece!!
It has lots of exclamation points!!
Don't worry about the quilt not being seamless.

I somehow like conjunctions
and prepositions
at beginnings of lines!

They are all serviceable
but i wonder if the A&M/UT one
is too regionally esoteric.

Grinning. Serviceable?
Don't get too enthusiastic!
Actually laughing.

That needs a comma after "actually."
I know this is very important to Texans
(and me), but it doesn't really qualify
as a holiday, does it?
Yes. It's called Thanksgiving.

Hence the Turkey in the name.

Drat. Passover is not Hanukkah.
Are there any "naturally green" beverages?!
I think we need to keep leprechauns
if they are associated with Christmas.

Other books from

Silver Boomer Books:

Anthologies:

Silver Boomers
   prose and poetry by and about baby boomers

Freckles to Wrinkles

This Path

From the Porch Swing
   memories of our grandparents

Flashlight Memories

The Harsh and the Heart
   Celebrating the Military

On Our Own
   Widowhood for Smarties

Single Author Books:

Song of County Roads
   by Ginny Greene

Crazy Lady in the Mirror
   by Madelyn Kamen

Books from

Eagle Wings Press
imprint of Silver Boomer Books

Slender Steps to Sanity
Twelve-Step Notes of Hope
by OAStepper, Compulsive Overeater

Writing Toward the Light
A Grief Journey
by Laura Flett

A Time for Verse
poetic ponderings on Ecclesiastes
by Barbara B. Rollins

Survived to Love
by Edward L. Hennessy (Ed H)

White Elephants
by Chynna T. Laird

A Cloud of Witnesses
Two Big Books and Us
by Barbara B. Rollins with OAStepper

Insights from the Jobsite
by Robyn Conley

you do. Live out your life and your traditions on your own terms. If it

Books from

Laughing Cactus Press
imprint of Silver Boomer Books

Poetry Floats
New and selected Philosophy-lite
by Jim Wilson

Bluebonnets, Boots and Buffalo Bones
by Sheryl L. Nelms

not so GRIMM
gentle fables and cautionary tales
by Becky Haigler

Three Thousand Doors
by Karen Elaine Greene

Milagros
by Tess Almendárez Lojacono

CPSIA information can be obtained at www.ICGtesting.com
Printed in the USA
LVOW120743080912

297954LV00001B/1/P